# Dead Serious

# DEAD SERIOUS

*A Book
for Teenagers
about
Teenage Suicide*
by
Jane Mersky Leder

ATHENEUM
*New York*

Atheneum
Macmillan Publishing Company
866 Third Avenue, New York, NY 10022

Composition by Haddon Craftsmen, Allentown, Pennsylvania
Printed and bound by Fairfield Graphics, Fairfield, Pennsylvania
Designed by Mary Ahern
First Edition

10   9   8   7   6   5   4   3   2

Library of Congress Cataloging-in-Publication Data

Leder, Jane Mersky.      Dead serious.

Bibliography: p. 143
SUMMARY: Discusses the problem of teenage suicide,
its effect on friends and family, warning signals, ways
of coping, and methods of helping a friend who is
considering suicide. Includes case histories, interviews
with teens who have attempted suicide, and a list
of places to turn for help.
1. Youth—United States—Suicidal behavior.
2. Adolescent psychology—United States. 3. Suicide—
United States—Prevention. [1. Suicide] I. Title.
HV6546.L43 1987      362.2      86-25880
ISBN 0-689-31262-8

*To my brother*
*Robin,*
*whose suicide caused me*
*to write this book*
*and whose spirit guided me*
*through it*

# Contents

*vii*

# Acknowledgments

To the special people whose energy and support helped me write this book: Jerry Cleaver, giver of "The Voice"; Marcia Marshall, believer in "The Voice"; Dr. Mary Giffin, a guiding force; Nancy Bohaboy and members of Buffalo Grove High School's peer counseling group; Karen Gunderson and the staff at Chicago's Barclay Hospital; Colonel Ted Atwood and the friends of Ted Atwood and Amy Pintarelli; Anthony Wiggins; Florea Dersam; Ernest, Carol, Elaine, Amy, and Paul Fluder; Dixie Logue; Ronald and Beverly Geske; Brian Wydra; Father Charles Rubey and the members of LOSS (Loving Outreach to Survivors of Suicide); Natalie Ruby; Lil Scalise; and my family . . . Shirley, Morris, Liz, John, Alan, and Joshua.

Some of the names in this book
have been changed in cases where the people referred to
would prefer to remain anonymous.

*A fire is cold compared to the fever that rises each day in my head*
*Day reaches for night and*
*Night becomes the day*
*In that manner I pray*
*God grant me the power to reach for my glory*
*And the key mystically moves with my will . . .*
*If death be life*
*As life is death*
*I yearn that coming with all my might*
*Let me see the light*
*that burns within me*
*For I cannot withstand the pain.*

Robin Mersky

# Dead Serious

# ( 1 )

## *When It's Someone You Know*

**K**EVIN'S HISTORY BOOK was open and sitting upright on his desk. He couldn't concentrate, not after last night's scene. He wondered whether Brad had gone straight home or walked the streets brooding over Olivia. Never mind. He and Brad were going to have a ball over the summer. Camp out on weekends. Work at the grocery down the street during the week and make some big bucks. Maybe take a trip to the Rockies at the end of the summer. Brad would forget all about Olivia and her stupid boyfriend. Kevin would make sure of that.

He closed his eyes. Thinking about his summer plans with Brad made him even more anxious for the school day to end. He needed to talk to Brad. They had a lot to work out.

When Kevin opened his eyes, he saw his counselor, Ms. Davies, standing over him.

"I need to talk to you," she said quietly.

What had he done now? Slowly, he picked up his books and followed Ms. Davies into the hall.

"Something terrible has happened to Brad," she said. "His mother found him in his car in the family garage last night."

*So, that's where he went.*

Ms. Davies took a deep breath. "Brad is dead. He took his own life."

"He's not dead," Kevin said calmly. "We're playing cards tonight."

Ms. Davies bit her upper lip. "I can imagine how you feel."

The funny thing was, he didn't feel a thing.

"There's a detective in Mrs. Lyons's office waiting to talk to you. He wants to ask you some questions."

"We're playing cards tonight. We always play on Friday," Kevin insisted.

KEVIN SLAMMED the car into reverse and screeched down the driveway. He and his parents had been arguing all morning. His mother was worried sick that he'd "drive off a cliff." His dad had ordered him not to drive to the funeral alone. They were upset. He didn't care. His best friend Brad was dead. The thought of him sitting in the garage in a car with the motor running, waiting to die, made Kevin shudder.

Why hadn't Brad talked about it? Kevin would have listened. They told each other everything. Now he wasn't sure. Maybe Brad hadn't wanted help. Maybe he hadn't wanted anyone to change his mind. Kevin swiped at the tears running down his cheeks. He wasn't going to get all choked up. Not again. Brad hadn't talked to him, so why should he care?

The funeral was supposed to be small, but there were hundreds of people, people Kevin had never seen before. He hated all the strangers. Brad would have hated them, too. He was the shy, quiet type who loved being by himself, taking things apart and putting them back together. Why couldn't he have gotten his life right? Kevin took a few steps toward the casket and stopped. He wasn't ready. Not yet. Besides, Brad wasn't really in there. It was someone's grandfather, someone old and sick. Brad was too young to die.

Kevin walked closer to the casket. He could see Brad's mom surrounded by a ring of people. She looked so tiny. Kevin had always thought of her as much taller. He remembered the night Brad had come home drunk. Mrs. Brogan had told Brad what a fool he was. If he wanted to be a fool, she'd said, he could be one on his own time. But he had better not be a fool in front of her again or she'd knock him around the block and back. Mrs. Brogan had seemed very tall that night.

Kevin wanted to talk to her. He wanted to tell her how sorry he was and how Brad chain-smoked when he played cards with the guys but never touched a cigarette in front of her. If only he could reach out and hug her and make everything like it was. But he could barely remember the last time he had hugged his own mother.

He found a seat. But he heard only bits of the minister's sermon. " . . . take solace in the fact that Brad, desperately confused and unhappy in life, has found eternal peace and happiness in the arms of the Lord."

The knot in his stomach tightened. Brad had had a

few problems. Who didn't? His girl friend Olivia had started dating someone else. Brad had cried when he'd found out. Olivia was the first girl friend he had ever had. And he hadn't been able to decide what to do after high school. Being a cook in Miami sounded cool. "Asshole idea," his dad had said.

When people started out to the parking lot, Kevin sat up, adjusted his tie, and nodded at the other three pallbearers standing near the casket. He had never understood funerals. His mother had told him that they make a permanent picture in your head that the dead person is gone. He didn't need a funeral to do that.

He moved from the foot of the casket, along the side, up to the head. He stared down at the body that didn't look a thing like his best friend. What had the mortician done? Brad's once-muscular chest was almost concave. His stomach looked like a beach ball ready to explode. Why couldn't they have left him alone? He jammed his fists into his suit pockets and turned away.

As the last of the guests left the chapel, the funeral director closed the casket and motioned for the pallbearers to come forward. He felt relieved. He knew Brad felt better, too.

Mrs. Brogan broke the silence. "I don't want it closed," she said, tugging at the lid of the casket. "Let me see him one more time."

"You've got to let go," Mr. Brogan pleaded. "Please don't. . . ."

"It's easy for you. You've had a lot of practice letting go. You never gave him what he needed."

"For God's sake, leave the casket be."

Kevin stood and watched in horror. Couldn't they wait?

There had to be a reason why Brad had killed himself. *Someone* was responsible. Not Mrs. Brogan. She had always been there when Brad needed her. And sometimes when he didn't. He remembered the time years before when she'd marched Brad back to the grocery store and made him admit to the checker that he'd lied when he said the eleven pop bottles were his. What he had done was dishonest, and Mrs. Brogan had wanted her son to accept the consequences. At the time, Brad had hated his mom for being so principled. Later on, he'd realized that what she'd done was right.

Kevin tried not to blame Mr. Brogan, but it wasn't easy. Brad's father worked, slept, and drank beer. That was it. When Brad had been younger, his dad had come to watch him play football. But when Brad had quit the team, his dad had been angry. "You're just like me, only worse," he had said. Brad wasn't anything like his dad. When his dad got angry, everyone paid. When Brad got angry, he got quiet and withdrawn. He was the only one who paid.

Kevin's best friend was dead, and there was no reason. If he'd died from a disease or an accident . . . . But he had killed himself. What could have been so bad? It made no sense.

He spent hours sitting on his bed listening to the same record. Sometimes he was certain that the footsteps he heard approaching his room were Brad's. Just like old times. But it was never Brad. He'd never see him again. That was the worst part. Never again.

Brad and he had grown up together, living two houses apart for over fifteen years. Now Kevin was alone. It wasn't fair. *Oh, God, just bring him back. I'll never do anything bad again.*

If only he had known Brad was so unhappy. If only he had seen the signs. But what signs?

Kevin remembered the night back in seventh grade after the roller-skating party. Brad and another friend, Dave, decided to walk home instead of riding the bus. They didn't have far to go. Besides, maybe they'd stop at McDonald's for something to eat. As the boys approached the restaurant, Brad challenged Dave to a race. Brad took off across Madison Street with Dave on his heels.

They only talked about the accident a couple of times. Brad told Kevin the car swerved to miss him but hit Dave instead. There was nothing the paramedics could do; Dave was dead on arrival at Good Shepherd Hospital.

Brad wasn't the same after that. He seemed to crawl into a shell. He got headaches that made him vomit, and his skin turn white. He got pimples all over his face. Kevin figured Brad had to work it out on his own; he didn't know what else to do.

If only he had done something then, maybe Brad would be alive now. If he had made him talk about it. But Brad had said he didn't want to talk, and Kevin hadn't pushed. Anyway, Brad couldn't have killed himself because of an accident so many years ago. He had to have forgotten all about it.

A sharp guy like Brad doesn't kill himself for no good reason. That would be crazy. Brad might have been confused, but he wasn't crazy. Maybe his dad had finally gotten to him. The two had never really gotten along except when Brad played on the football team. After he quit, his dad was always cutting him down, telling him he'd better "wake up and smell the coffee before it's too late."

Mr. Brogan was a cop who worked the shift from three in the afternoon to eleven at night. And on weekends, Mr. Brogan sat in front of the TV, drinking beer and doing crossword puzzles. If he drank too much, and he often did, he'd either fall asleep or leave the house without telling anyone where he was going.

One night, the phone rang late, and it was someone from the hospital telling Mrs. Brogan that her husband had been in an accident and that she had better come right away. Brad said the one side of his dad's face had looked like it had been mashed in a blender. He was cut up so badly that he stayed in the hospital for almost a week.

"That's not good enough," Kevin screamed. "You couldn't have killed yourself because of your old man. You could have moved out, gotten your own place with some other guys.–You go off and kill yourself without letting me know, without letting me help. Okay. So you wanted to keep it to yourself. Fine. Keep it *all* to yourself. I don't care. Just don't expect me to waste my tears over you." Tears streamed down his face.

Maybe it was Olivia. Maybe this was all her fault. She and Brad broke up every other week. They broke up, then got back together. Again and again. They went steady off and on for two and a half years.

Brad and Olivia would be going separate ways after graduation. So why not get it over with? Brad didn't care. At least that's what he said. But when he heard Olivia was dating someone else, he started to cry. He picked up the phone and asked her out. She said no. Brad didn't go out with girls after that. He played cards with Kevin and the other guys instead.

"You're lucky," he said to Kevin during a card game.

"You know what you want to do. You've got your art. You want to be an artist. I've got nothing."

Kevin felt uncomfortable. He knew Brad was having a hard time. "You'll get it together," he said.

Brad stared into space.

He called Olivia again. He wanted to see her. She said okay, but bring Kevin along. When the two got to Olivia's, she was with her new boyfriend and some other guy. Without saying a word, Brad turned and stormed out the front door. Olivia followed.

"I figured this would happen," the new boyfriend said.

"He's upset," Kevin mumbled.

He hated Olivia for setting this up. What was she trying to prove?

After what seemed like hours, Brad and Olivia came back.

"Let's split," Brad said. Kevin took one look at him and knew he meant business.

Outside, Brad insisted on walking home. "Just go. Take my car and go."

"I can't take your car."

"Take it," he said, shoving the keys into Kevin's hand.

"Come on, this is nuts." Kevin tried to give the keys back. But Brad had already turned around and begun walking away.

Frustrated, Kevin got into the car, turned the key in the ignition, and slowly backed down the driveway. Okay, he thought, I'll cruise around the block a few times and stall for time. Brad needs to cool off.

After wasting several minutes, he drove by Brad walking slowly toward home.

"Hey, jump in. You're crazy to walk. Besides, this is your car."

"I want to walk. Just park the car in the driveway and leave the keys in the mailbox."

No use arguing. When Brad made up his mind to do something, he did it. No point in trying to stop him.

A MONTH AFTER Brad killed himself, Kevin halfheartedly agreed to play poker with some of the guys. He had to get out of the house.

Slouched in his chair, he reached for each of the five cards dealt to him. A king and ten of diamonds. He'd keep those. A two of hearts, seven of clubs, queen of spades. Those he'd discard. He slammed the three cards down on the table. Just then, something very strange happened. He smelled the sweet fragrance of roses all around him. But there were no roses in the room. And he started to shiver, even though it was a very warm summer night. *It's you, Brad, isn't it?* He was breathless. *You're here, aren't you?* He glanced nervously at the other guys. Did they feel Brad's presence, too?

*Okay, it's just you and me.* A shiver ran up his spine. *You really botched things up. Caused a lot of grief around here. Your mom is having a real hard time. And I miss you so much.* Kevin swallowed hard; he didn't want to start to cry. Not now, with the other guys around.

Kevin blinked. He couldn't believe what he saw. There, standing in front of him, was Brad. He was sure of it. Cautiously, he reached out to touch him. Too late. Brad had already turned from him and started to walk away.

After that night, Kevin read everything he could about death and dying. He had to know whether he was crazy or not. Had he really seen Brad or was it all a figment of his imagination? Combing through a book about death, he found a section on the Hindus and their beliefs. It said that the Hindus believe that the soul of a dead person floats around right after death, trying to make contact with those it loved. It also said that the soul of someone who takes his own life floats around even longer. Kevin was relieved. It *had been* Brad he'd seen. He wasn't crazy after all.

Kevin waited anxiously to see Brad again. He had so much to tell him. He was going to art school in the fall. The high-school baseball team had taken the league championship. Olivia and her new boyfriend had broken up.

He organized more poker games, hoping that Brad would show up again. He never did. He tried staying up all night, afraid Brad wouldn't be able to wake him if he were sound asleep. After five sleepless nights, he gave in and slept thirteen hours straight.

Weeks turned into months. He never saw Brad again. But he thought about him a lot. Some days he thought he understood why Brad had killed himself; other days he had no idea. He could never remember how long it had been since Brad had died. Sometimes it seemed like years, sometimes only a few days.

Time was meaningless to Brad's mom, too. She and Kevin talked a lot. Every time he saw her, she cried. Not right away. She pretended she was fine at the beginning. Then she'd ask Kevin if he remembered a certain incident such as the time she'd marched Brad to the grocery store to return the bottle money. And then she'd cry. At first, Kevin felt funny talking about Brad. He thought the less he talked, the sooner the pain would end. But it was just the opposite. Talking made him feel better. Sometimes it made him laugh. More often, it made him cry. The letting go felt good. But the searching for answers never stopped.

THE KNOT in Kevin's stomach loosens. His younger brother tells a dumb joke about the chicken crossing the road and he laughs. The wounds are starting to heal. And sometimes things are almost as they were. He forgets all about Brad. The pain is gone. Then, like a ghost, it attacks. Playing baseball on a hot summer afternoon, opening a bedroom dresser drawer and finding an old shirt he once loaned to Brad. How could he ever forget?

———

SUICIDE affects many more people than just the teenager who gases or hangs him- or herself. It affects the entire family and many friends. While the suicide victim's pain has ended, the pain for suicide survivors has just begun. It can last a lifetime.

Everyone reacts differently to a friend's suicide. Some people scream and cry. Others, like Kevin, don't show any emotion at first. They're too numb. It's all a bad dream. But sooner or later, they're forced to accept the truth: A friend is dead, and the death was *not* a mistake.

Accepting death is never easy. Accepting a friend's suicide is even more difficult. It may take years. While everyone reacts and feels differently, there are some common responses. Friends (parents, siblings, and relatives, too) may experience some or all of these feelings during the months following a suicide.

EARLY REACTIONS AND FEELINGS

*Frantic Activity*

In order to keep their minds off what has happened, some people fill their time with what seems like frantic activity. They keep themselves busy from morning to night so they don't have time to think.

*Confusion*

Why? Why? Why? For many, the suicide begins a search for answers . . . a search that can rarely be satisfied.

*Guilt*

Friends, like Kevin, feel they could have prevented the suicide if only they had known how unhappy their friend was. Or, in some cases, they knew their friend was suicidal but didn't tell anyone, probably because they were sworn to secrecy. Now they are left behind, carrying the guilt of not having done all they could have done.

*Anger*

Anger because the friend didn't discuss what she was going to do. . . .

Anger because suicide is such an unacceptable way of solving problems. . . .

Anger because the suicide has left so many people unhappy.

*Fear*

Once a friend has died by suicide, it's normal to fear that someone else . . . maybe even yourself . . . will try to kill him- or herself. Suicides often occur in clusters, or groups, with one suicide "giving permission" for others to take their own lives. Suicide can be catching. Kids who are depressed and sitting on the fence don't need much of a push. The suicide death of one young person makes it easier for the next one.

### LATER REACTIONS AND FEELINGS

*Blame*

It's not unusual to look for someone to blame. Brad's mother blamed his father. Kevin blamed Brad's father and his girl friend Olivia. Blaming, of course, doesn't change a thing. Suicide is a decision that comes from within when someone finds the idea of dying less painful than continuing to live.

*Idolizing*

Sometimes it's easier to remember a suicide victim as "perfect," as someone who could do no wrong. The problem here is that such feelings may make it harder to deal honestly with the death.

*Sensing One's Own Mortality*

When a friend dies, it makes death very real and reminds all of the survivors that they, too, will die. Some people may become very careful in everything they do. Others may start taking risks to "tempt fate" and prove that *they* aren't going to die.

*Hope*

Finally, friends are able to begin to have hope for the future. They realize that their lives will go on. And they may have learned some valuable lessons from such a terrible experience.

IF YOU KNOW SOMEONE who has died by suicide and feel that you need help or information, contact any of the following people or organizations near you:

1. Local mental health agency
2. Local health department
3. Suicide support groups
4. Clergy
5. Private counselors

# (2)

# Lives with the Tears Washed Away: Statistics and Causes

TO KEVIN and all the others who knew and loved him, Brad's suicide serves as a constant reminder of how precious life is. To the statisticians who keep the numbers on suicide, Brad is just another statistic. He is one of approximately five thousand American teenagers (thirteen-to nineteen-year-olds) who kill themselves every year. More than any other group of people in the world, American teens have the greatest opportunity to grow and prosper. Yet an alarming number of your peers are choosing to die instead.

Every day, an average of eighteen teens kill themselves. Every hour, fifty-seven children and young adults in the United States *try* to kill themselves—well over a thousand a day. Every year, an estimated one million young Americans move in and out of suicidal crisis.

The teenage years can be rough. Even in the best of times, you are faced with an avalanche of changes and expectations. Parents expect you to become an independent person, capable of making your own decisions and taking care of yourself. Teachers and parents expect you to decide what to do after graduation and how to do it. Your friends expect you to fit in. As if that's not enough, your body is experiencing great physical and biochemical changes. One minute you are elated; the next you feel depressed.

It's not surprising that the teen years are often filled with fear, loneliness, and insecurity. What *is* surprising is the fact that teenagers today seem less able or less willing to cope with the same changes and expectations their parents faced not so long ago.

According to one study of seven thousand high school students, one out of every five teens reported severe problems with self-esteem, feelings of failure, alienation, loneliness, lack of self-confidence, low self-regard, and thoughts of suicide. Researchers in Chicago who surveyed teens in the late 1970s and in 1980 found that 20 percent of them felt emotionally empty and confused most of the time, more interested in dying than living. And in researching a book on teenage rebellion, Reverend Truman Dollar and psychiatrist Grace Ketterman discovered that 34 percent of the teens questioned said they had seriously considered suicide; 32 percent said they had made specific plans to take their lives; and an astounding 14 percent said they had attempted suicide! There are apparently more teens thinking, obsessing, and worrying about suicide than ever before.

Suicide is officially the second-biggest killer of young people behind accidents. Yet many experts are convinced that suicide is really the number one killer. They feel that many of the accident victims are suicides in disguise. Because the stigma attached to suicide is so great, officials as well as parents often report that a suicide was an accident. If the victim does not leave a suicide note or other proof that his or her death was intentional, the death might be intentionally or wrongly ruled an accident or a homicide.

Car accidents, for example, account for about 37 percent of all deaths in the fifteen- to twenty-four-year-old age group. Of these deaths, experts speculate that approximately 25 percent are intentional. The victims committed autocide; they caused their own deaths by driving recklessly with the intent of dying. However, because there is no way of proving that these deaths were intentional, they go down in the record books as accidents.

There is no doubt that the true number of teen suicides is much higher than the official statistics report. But the official statistics are all we have, and they are disturbing enough. The rate of teen suicide tripled between 1955 and 1975. The rate almost doubled between 1965 and 1975. And between 1975 and 1982—the most recent figures we have—the rate of teen suicide continued to increase, particularly for young males between the ages of fifteen and nineteen.

WHY ARE MORE TEENS KILLING THEMSELVES?

The plain but simple truth is that no one knows why teenagers kill themselves. The suicide victims aren't around to tell us, and they probably couldn't, anyway. The experts have all kinds of possible theories, but there is no way of knowing for sure. Chances are that there are many causes leading to a teen suicide—maybe as many as twelve to fifteen. Contrary to what you may have thought, someone like Brad doesn't kill himself because his girl friend broke up with him. Olivia's rejection may have been the "straw that broke the camel's back," but there were many other problems that contributed to Brad's decision to take his own life.

### BLOCKED COMMUNICATION

Brad's dad is in some ways a typical American father. He spent little time with his son while Brad was growing up. When they were together, Brad and his father had trouble communicating. Mr. Brogan denied that Brad had any problems and once said that his son was just like him, only a little worse. When Brad's friend, Dave, was killed, Mrs. Brogan suggested to her husband that Brad see a counselor to work out his hurt and guilt. Mr. Brogan refused the suggestion, saying Brad could solve his own problems. When Mrs. Brogan saw how sick Brad was with headaches and severe acne, she again suggested that Brad get help. Again, Mr. Brogan said no. He was unable to respond to his son's emotional injuries, convinced that Brad's problems were not serious.

Blocked communication between teens and their parents (or parent) is often a factor in suicide. Many suicidal teens feel they cannot talk to their parents (or to anyone else).

Brad tried to talk to his dad about his interest in working as a cook in Miami after graduation. Mr. Brogan told Brad that was an "asshole idea" and that "he should wake up and smell the coffee before it's too late." It didn't take very long for Brad to give up on his father as someone who could comfort and advise him.

Mr. Brogan was unable to see that Brad had problems. He felt that if he babied his son, Brad would never grow up. Mr. Brogan had survived his own teenage traumas. So would Brad.

### GROWING UP DEAD

Many suicidal teens cannot show anger or pain. They keep their emotions inside until they fester and explode. These teens might be described as "perfect children." They appear to be very happy on the outside, never disagreeing with their parents. Their only goal is to win their parents' love and approval. The best way to do that, they think, is not to cause trouble, even if it means keeping important feelings to themselves forever.

These teens "grow up dead," cutting off their emotions, their demands, and their personalities. They cannot communicate honestly with their parents (or with anyone else). Because they feel as if they're already dead, the idea of suicide doesn't frighten them as much as it would others.

### PARENTS BEHAVING LIKE CHILDREN

Some teens come to see suicide as the only way to eliminate the stress of living with parents who behave more like children than adults. In these families, the child is expected to take care of the parent (parents), to constantly give help and advice. Such a reversal in the parent/child roles puts tremendous pressure on the child. The child, instead of the parent, feels responsible for solving problems. He or she spends most of his or her time trying to figure out what mood the parent is in. Children put in this position often feel hopeless and worthless. They blame themselves for family problems. Taught to rely only on themselves, these kids are forced to grow up without the loving guidance of their parents.

Natalie attempted suicide twice. Her mother was a manic-depressive who had been in and out of hospitals for years. Natalie grew up without her mother's support and supervision. Instead, she often had to look after her. When she didn't take her medication, Natalie's mother was like a child.

Natalie was always on her guard around her mother. She never knew what her mother's mood would be and how she would act. She was afraid to bring friends home.

### LOSS

Many teens who commit suicide suffer the loss of someone or something very important. A parent, friend, or sibling dies. Parents get divorced. A mother goes back to work full time. Whatever the loss, it makes life empty and lonely.

You'll recall that when Brad's friend was hit and killed by a speeding car, Brad seemed to crawl into a shell. As Kevin put it, "He just wasn't the same after that." Brad lost interest in everyone and everything. And he developed bad headaches and a severe case of acne. Kevin tried to help Brad by talking about the accident, but Brad wouldn't talk much. Mrs. Brogan suggested Brad see a counselor; Mr. Brogan refused. Brad was left to come to terms with his friend's death alone. And, although no one will ever know for sure, it is quite possible that he never really accepted what had happened. Brad had told Kevin that the car swerved to miss him and hit Dave instead.

Maybe Brad felt that he should have been the one who was killed.

Mrs. Brogan talked about the legal proceedings that dragged on for almost two years after the accident. Dave's parents wanted the driver of the car prosecuted and they wanted Brad to testify as the main witness. Brad was frightened.

"Why are Dave's parents doing this?" he asked his mother.

"They're angry," she said.

"What are they going to do with the money?"

"The money isn't important. They just want the driver to be held responsible."

"If they don't win, are they going to blame me?"

As it turned out, Dave's parents settled the case out of court. Brad was never called to testify.

Ten weeks before Brad killed himself, Dave's father died suddenly of a brain hemorrhage. Kevin and other friends noticed that Brad talked about Dave more than he ever had before. Mrs. Brogan feels that the death of Dave's father opened up more memories than Brad could handle, forcing him to relive the accident all over again.

DIVORCE

Divorce is another factor in teen suicides. The United States has the highest divorce rate in the world, with one out of every two marriages failing. Many young suicides are children of divorce or homes where there are serious problems.

Brad's parents spent little time together. Mr. Brogan worked the night shift; Mrs. Brogan worked days. On weekends, Mr. Brogan like to watch television, do crossword puzzles, and drink beer. He rarely agreed to do anything with the family. The tension between Brad's parents grew over the years. So did the stress between Brad and his father. Mrs. Brogan remembers a conversation she and Brad had.

"Was my father different?" he asked her.

"What do you mean?"

"Before—when you married him."

"No," she said.

"Then why did you marry him? You're so different."

Brad was clearly aware of the tension between his parents. No matter how hard the Brogans may have tried to hide their differences, they were unsuccessful. Brad must have felt torn by his parents' problems. Although he sided with his mother, Brad loved his father, too, and longed for his parents to work out their difficulties.

No matter how much he may have wished for reconciliation, Brad couldn't do a thing about his parents' failing marriage. Mr. Brogan's drinking and seeming lack of interest in his family eroded any trust Mrs. Brogan still had in him and in the marriage. The Brogans separated six months after Brad's death and are now divorced.

If Brad had not killed himself and lived through his parents' divorce, he most likely would have feared that he was somehow responsible. Because he probably would have continued to live with his mother, Brad might have had to listen to Mrs. Brogan's bitterness toward her ex-husband. She might have labeled him the "bad guy," and Brad, having been told he was just like his dad, only worse, would have felt like a louse.

For many teens, divorce is harder to accept than death. Whether the single parent is a "good" mother or father, the mechanics of bringing home a paycheck, cooking, cleaning, disciplining, and befriending are a heavy load. The amount of time and attention given to children in the home is limited. The support system is shaky at best. Kids don't see two adults struggling to work out problems. As a result, children living with single parents often grow up expecting that problems can be solved quickly and without much struggle. When their own problems don't get settled overnight, these kids can get very depressed, convinced that their pain will last forever.

Never before in the history of any society has there been a situation in which only one person is left with the responsibility of raising children. The effects are devastating, with the rise in teen suicide parallel to the rise in the divorce rate.

"LOVE ON THE BONUS PLAN"

Many suicidal teens have parents who seem loving and concerned but who are determined to mold their children into the kind of people *they* want them to be. Mr. Brogan, for example, wanted Brad to be a star athlete. As long as Brad played on the school football team, his father showed his support and enthusiasm by going to the games. But when Brad decided to quit the team, Mr. Brogan was obviously disappointed. He withdrew what little love he was able to show. The message from Mr. Brogan was clear: If you aren't going to succeed as an athlete, I won't love you.

In the last weeks of his life, Ted, a senior in high school, drew fantasy cartoons and recorded his thoughts in a secret code that only a close friend could decipher. *My choices are to run away or to commit suicide,* one message was decoded to read.

Ted, the son of a retired lieutenant colonel in the U.S. Army, was thoughtful and articulate. He loved long debates about evolution versus creation. He impressed his friends with his understanding of things, such as how speed affects time. Even though he got $B$'s and $C$'s, Ted's aptitude scores put him near the top of his class. Because of this promise as a student and as a future officer in the armed forces (he was active in his high school's ROTC program), Ted received a presidential nomination to compete for admission to West Point.

But the pressure of trying to improve his $B$ and $C$ grades in order to apply to West Point made Ted extremely unhappy. He confided to a friend that he didn't know if he could live up to his parents' expectations. It was clear they wanted him to attend West Point; Ted wasn't sure he belonged there. Slowly, he just gave up on his studies. He stopped doing homework and did poorly on an important test four days before his death. It really hurt him to fail, and he told a friend after he got his grade that he needed psychiatric help. The friend didn't think Ted was serious. He just laughed it off.

Stuffed in his locker at school, police investigators found a strange story Ted had written. It was called: "The Push . . . the Fear. . . ." In it, Ted was talking about his good and bad traits. One was "fear of failure." Next to it he wrote: *Oh, hey, you coward.*

Ted taped a garden hose to the exhaust pipe of his car and ran it inside through a window. With the engine running, he sat with his feet on the dashboard and waited to die.

Many experts feel a teen's most important job is to learn how to handle tension and to take responsibility for his or her own behavior and values. But when the pressures to achieve and succeed are loaded on top of the normal stresses a teen faces, self-esteem and self-reliance can collapse.

With the pressure to succeed overwhelming him, Ted, like many other teens, became frightened and gave up. He was unable to function and became very depressed. He knew he was going to disappoint his parents; he couldn't face his "failure."

Part of Ted's coded obituary, written shortly before he killed himself, read:

> *My IQ is 142*
> *My mind is diseased      That I know*
> *I am going to kill myself*
> *What a relief it was*
> *I am so much better now*
> *You cannot do wrong when you are dead*
> *Time is infinite      You are at the beginning*

———

"THIS IS THE ONLY THING AROUND HERE THAT HAS ANY ROOTS"
After moving into a third house in a third different city, Ron T. hanged himself from the branch of a tree in his backyard and left a note: "This is the only thing around here that has any roots."

When David Beres was five, his family moved from Ohio to Michigan. As the new kid on the block, he was picked on by the other children. Some of the bigger kids threw pebbles at him. He would run home crying but stopped just before he walked in the front door. He told his dad that he felt sorry for a child that others were picking on. He never said that the child was himself.

When David started high school, he was picked on again. One upperclassman apparently said, "I'm going to kill you." And another boy, the day before what was called "Nerd Day" at school, told David, "You don't have to dress like a nerd tomorrow because you *are* one."

Later the next day, David hanged himself with a noose made from two straps from his and his brother's backpacks. Police investigators listed "peer teasing" as one of the possible precipitating causes of his suicide.

With so many Americans on the move, neighborhoods and schools are different from the way they used to be. Fifty or sixty years ago, most Americans lived in rural areas and stayed put their entire lives. The community was strong. People cared for each other. The roots were deep.

Today, 80 percent of Americans live in cities, and they move often from one city to another. Between March 1983 and March 1984, the period for which the most recent figures are available, 39.4 million Americans moved to a different residence. Neighborhoods aren't the same. They're always changing. Many people don't even know their neighbors. That makes it tough on everyone.

It's easy to feel insecure and alone. If your situation is like that of many teens, both of your parents work outside of the home. You usually come home after school to an empty house. And even when your parents are home, they're often busy. The statistics say that you spend an average of just fourteen minutes a week talking with your parents. You spend a lot more time in front of the TV set. By the time you graduate from high school, you will have seen twenty thousand hours of television and almost the same number of killings. You will have been taught that problems are solved in the space of thirty minutes and that everyone ends up happy.

So, what's the solution? What can you do to feel more secure and involved? Maybe you can sign up for sports or other afterschool activities. Maybe you can tell your parents that you want to spend more time together. Maybe you can channel your energies to solving serious problems like pollution, corruption, or the threat of nuclear war. And, most of all, maybe you can understand that problems aren't usually solved overnight but with time and patience. The more involved you are with people and activities you like and enjoy, the better your chances of not getting swallowed up by loneliness and insecurity.

### BONDING

Vivienne Loomis was fourteen when she hanged herself in her mother's empty silversmithing studio. According to her mother, Vivienne made very few demands as a baby. She was quiet and could be left alone in her playpen for long periods of time. Because her two older children were much more active, Mrs. Loomis was grateful that Vivienne seemed to need so little time and attention. As she looks back, Mrs. Loomis feels Vivienne was "seriously injured by being left alone so much."

When Vivienne was two, her parents and older brother went to Europe for ten weeks. Vivienne and her sister were left with a baby-sitter who had stayed with the children before. When her parents returned from their trip, Vivienne didn't seem to recognize her mother and had nothing to do with her for several days. While her reaction was quite normal for a young child, by the time Vivienne was three, she had tuned her mother out.

When Robin was eighteen months old, he woke from

a nap in terrible pain. His right arm was paralyzed, and he had a very high fever. His mother rushed Robin to the hospital where doctors took him, screaming, for tests and observation. His mother pleaded with the hospital staff to let her stay with her son. She tried to explain that she and Robin had never been separated. The staff sent her home. Frantic, she called the hospital all night long to check on Robin's condition. By morning, Robin had regained the use of his arm, and the fever had broken. His illness was diagnosed as a case of twenty-four-hour polio. When his mother asked about further treatment, she was told there was none. Robin was no longer contagious, the doctors said, but should be kept in the hospital for further observation. His mother refused and signed the necessary papers to have Robin released.

Before Robin went into the hospital, he was a talkative, well-adjusted child. When he came home, he had stopped talking. He didn't utter a word for months. He refused to look at his mother. He screamed when he saw anyone dressed in white. And he had terrible nightmares, screaming hysterically when he woke. The trauma of being separated from his mother and kept in isolation in a hospital overnight left an indelible mark on him.

From then until Robin was much older, he had a very difficult time being away from his mother. She eventually made an agreement with the nursery school Robin was to attend. She would take him there, and, if he wanted to stay, he would.

Years later, Robin stuck a hunting rifle into his mouth and pulled the trigger. He died instantly.

What did Robin and Vivienne have in common? Was there something that happened to both of them as young children, which may have contributed to their suicides years later?

As an infant, Vivienne spent very little special time with her mother. She played alone in her playpen, while her mother took care of the other two children. Then, when Vivienne's parents went to Europe for ten weeks, she may have felt abandoned, left with a baby-sitter for such a long time.

Robin, too, was separated from his mother at a very early age. While the circumstances were different and the separation much shorter, it was still traumatic. He stopped talking, had terrible nightmares, and screamed whenever he saw anyone dressed in white.

Both Robin and Vivienne "lost" the most important person in their lives. They must have felt scared and alone. Where had their mothers gone? Why had they been abandoned? The horrifying experience of being separated from their mothers at such an early age may have set the base of their personalities, putting them on what one psychiatrist calls a "narrow fulcrum." Ordinary stresses tipped their sense of balance more easily than they do for others. This trait, in combination with many other events in their lives, may have led to Robin's and Vivienne's suicides.

### DEPRESSION

Up until twenty years ago, the medical profession as a whole did not believe that children and teenagers got depressed. They were convinced that childhood and adolescence were carefree times, times free of major problems. Only older people, they reasoned, could be depressed. How wrong they were! Study after study now confirms that depression is common in young people. As many as one in every five teenagers may be depressed. According to the National Association for Mental Health, nearly 20 percent of those who receive care for depression in hospitals and clinics are under the age of eighteen. And, while many young suicides did not seem depressed, depression now appears to be the single most common cause of teen suicide.

### THE GOOD NEWS ABOUT DEPRESSION

Only thirty years ago, shock therapy (or ECT—electroconvulsive therapy) was about all there was available to help the depressed. Today, there are new drugs called antidepressants, old drugs being used in different ways, expanded psychiatric services, light therapy, and sleep therapy, all of which aid the depressed in dramatic ways to deal better with their condition. According to the experts, well over 80 percent of depressed patients can be significantly helped. That's good news!

### KINDS OF DEPRESSION

There are at least six kinds of depression, ranging from unipolar depression—depression that usually lasts for a few months before lifting—to bipolar (manic) depression that causes its victims to go up and down in mood indefinitely. The most important thing to understand is that depression can range from the ordinary "downs" that everyone experiences at one time or another to crippling kinds that may require hospitalization.

### WHAT DOES IT FEEL LIKE
### TO BE DEPRESSED?

People describe depression differently. Some say that it's like living under a "black cloud." Others say that it's having a bad case of the "blues." However they describe it, those who have been depressed often share many of the same feelings:

1. *Sadness*—"I am so sad or unhappy that I can't stand it."
2. *Pessimism/hopelessness*—"I feel that the future is hopeless and that things will never improve."
3. *Guilt*—"I feel as though I am very bad or worthless."
4. *Self-dislike*—"I hate myself."
5. *Self-accusations*—"I blame myself for everything bad that happens."
6. *Suicidal ideas*—"I would kill myself if I could."

HOW CAN YOU TELL IF SOMEONE YOU KNOW IS DEPRESSED?

If someone you know is tired and unhappy, having trouble sleeping, not eating, and generally uninterested in doing much of anything, s/he may be depressed.

While someone who is depressed won't necessarily experience all of the following symptoms, s/he will experience at least four of them nearly every day for two weeks or more.

1. Change in appetite—eating less
2. Sleep disturbance—taking a long time to fall asleep and waking early
3. Loss of interest or pleasure in activities
4. Loss of energy, fatigue
5. Feelings of self-hatred, guilt, and worthlessness
6. Inability to think or concentrate
7. Inability to do much of anything
8. Recurrent thoughts of death or suicide

### WHAT CAUSES DEPRESSION?

There are often several reasons why someone may be depressed.

1. Not feeling loved or understood
2. Feeling rejected
3. Trouble with friends and family
4. Feeling "no good"
5. A loss (death, divorce, breakup with a girl friend/ boyfriend)
6. Anger
7. Chemical imbalance—There is increasing evidence that neurotransmitters related to the production of neurochemicals can be the cause of certain kinds of depression. The field of psychiatry is on the edge of chemical breakthroughs, too complicated for this book, but full of promise for the depressed.

### TREATING DEPRESSION: WHAT CAN BE DONE?

For many teens, a combination of psychotherapy— talking alone with a psychologist or psychiatrist—and family therapy is successful in treating depression.

For others, a combination of drug therapy (antidepressants) and talk therapy seems to work better. The key, say the leading psychologists, is flexibility. If a month or two go by and talk therapy isn't helping, it may be time to try drugs. Often talk therapy can help teens who are taking antidepressants recover even more quickly.

But treating depression doesn't stop there. Some teens get depressed only during the winter months when the days are short and the amount of sunlight is limited.

They suffer from a newly discovered kind of depression called Seasonal Affective Disorder (SAD), which makes them miserable. Treatment for SAD is simple: sitting in front of a special light fixture that looks like a large, glowing mirror for an hour or two in the morning and another hour at night. The fixture is equipped with fluorescent lights that include all the colors found in natural sunlight. Adding light to these depressed teens who are light-starved works wonders. Almost all of them who have been treated this way have improved quickly.

Sleep therapy has also proved successful in treating some depressed teens. Most depressed people take a long time to fall asleep and wake up hours earlier than others. The REM period of the night—the time when dreaming usually occurs—begins much earlier than normal and occurs most during the first third of the night, rather than during the last third, as is experienced by most healthy people.

Doctors can now use these differences in sleep patterns to decide if a person is depressed and to predict whether a certain antidepressant drug will work. They can also change sleep patterns to improve a patient's mood; they can reset the body clock.

A sixteen-year-old boy was sent to a sleep lab because of his worsening depression. He had been an honor student and star athlete but now fell asleep in class, couldn't do his work, lost his interest in sports, and talked about suicide. His sleep habits had changed dramatically in one year. He used to go to sleep at 11:00 P.M.; now he was unable to fall asleep until 3:00 A.M.

The first night of treatment, the boy went to bed at 3:00 A.M. and was awakened at 10:30 the next morning. The following day, he went to bed at 6:00 A.M. and was awakened at 12:30 in the afternoon. Within a week, he was falling asleep at 11:00 P.M. His body clock had been reset, and his fatigue and depression soon disappeared!

While not all teens who take their own lives are depressed, the breakthroughs in treating those who are promise a brighter future for the thousands of teenagers who get so down that death becomes the only way out.

# (3)

# *Gone with the Wind: A Case History*

I F SOMEONE you knew has died by suicide, chances are you've spent a lot of time trying to figure out why. You have searched for reasons to explain such an unacceptable death. You've retraced your friendship and then all the times—good and bad—that you and your friend spent together. You may have talked to your friend's parents and siblings, desperately trying to find some answers. Piecing together the life of one suicide victim—performing what is called a "psychological autopsy"—can often shed some light on what may have gone wrong.

———

TERI WAS dragging her feet. It was almost time for her parents to drive her the thirty-five miles to Northern Illinois University in DeKalb, and she still had last-minute errands to run. Maybe she'd put off buying school supplies as a silent protest against leaving home.

Teri stood in front of the school supplies at a local drugstore. "I don't know which pens to get," she said in a small, childlike voice.

Her older sister, Elaine, grabbed a handful of inexpensive ballpoints and tossed them into the shopping cart.

"And what about notebooks?" Teri asked. "I have no idea what kind to buy."

Elaine looked at her sister. Why was she having such a hard time making simple decisions? "I used these last year," she said, picking up several narrow-lined notebooks and throwing them on top of the pens.

Elaine felt sorry for Teri, remembering how scared she'd been the day she'd left for college.

"Need anything else?" she asked.

"I don't know what I need," Teri mumbled. "I just don't know."

Elaine was worried. It wasn't like Teri to be so indecisive. "What's wrong with you?" she asked. "What's the matter?"

"Nothing . . . nothing," Teri said, as she started pushing the cart down the aisle. "It's getting late. Let's go."

SAYING GOOD-BYE to Teri wasn't easy. Elaine sat staring at the driveway long after her sister and parents had pulled away. Teri had looked so lost, sitting there in the backseat of the car, smothered by all of her belongings. Elaine had let her down. She hadn't said the right things. Maybe she should have gone, too. She could have helped Teri unpack or walked around campus with her. But Teri might have been embarrassed. She might not have wanted her older sister tagging along. Elaine didn't know what to think. Part of her felt stupid for worrying so much; the other part knew instinctively that Teri needed her. It took about thirty minutes before she grabbed a jacket, got into her car, and headed for the university.

Teri was surprised to see Elaine but didn't say much as she unpacked. Her roommate had stopped in earlier, just long enough to drop off a load of her things. She'd gone home for more and wouldn't be back until later the following afternoon. Around six, Teri's parents decided it was time to leave. Knowing Elaine was planning to stay longer made it easier to say good-bye. Besides, they'd be seeing Teri in less than a week for a cousin's wedding.

After dinner at a campus restaurant, Elaine bought Teri a six-pack of beer and a pint of whiskey to take back to the dorm and share with some of the other girls. She figured that was a good way to get Teri to meet new people. Otherwise, Teri might stay alone in her room like Elaine had done when she'd first gone away to school.

"I'll stay longer if you want," Elaine said, knowing how frightened Teri was.

"No, I'll be fine."

Elaine slowly tied her jacket around her waist, giving Teri time to change her mind.

"Sure you don't want me to stay?" she asked again, putting her arms around Teri and holding her tight. She couldn't stop the tears streaming down her cheeks.

"I'm sure," Teri said, sobbing softly.

Twenty minutes out of DeKalb, Elaine pulled over on the side of the road and stopped the car. Maybe she should turn around and go back. Teri hadn't really wanted her to leave. She'd just said that to look brave. Was she just overreacting because of her own insecurities the year before? Or did Teri really need her? She'd made the offer to stay. Teri had turned her down. She was probably okay. Most likely she'd gone across the hall and was beginning to relax and have some fun. The other girls would cheer her up. Elaine made up her mind not to turn around.

Elaine stayed home the next day, waiting to hear from Teri. She never called. At six, as the family was eating dinner, a local policeman rang the doorbell. Teri's mother went to the door. The policeman told her as gently as he could that Teri was dead.

In order to lessen the shock for her other children, Teri's mother said that Teri had died accidentally from an overdose of drugs and alcohol. Only after the funeral were Elaine and the others told what had really happened: Teri had gone into the closet, sat on a box, taken the drawstring of her laundry bag, which was hanging on a hook, and put it around her neck, then leaned forward. Her roommate had found her late the next afternoon. The coroner estimated that she had been dead since midnight. She had been legally drunk when she'd died.

Guilt swept over Elaine like ocean waves during a raging storm. Alcohol was part of what had killed Teri, and Elaine had bought the booze. She had killed her own sister. How could she ever get through the rest of her life knowing what she had done? She fell apart, lying in bed at night, sobbing uncontrollably. "Why did you do it, Teri?" she cried into the darkness. "Why didn't you ask me for help?" Over and over again, Elaine blamed herself for buying the alcohol and for not turning back.

AS YOUNG NEWLYWEDS, Carol and Ernie Fluder dreamed of having a large family. Carol would leave her job as a nurse to stay home with the kids, while Ernie pursued his career as a mechanical engineer. Exactly eleven months after her wedding night, the first of her five children, Elaine, was born. Elaine was a happy baby who held her parents' undivided attention for all of sixteen months until Teresa (Teri, for short) was born. Just over a year later, a third baby girl, Laura, arrived. Carol had her hands full with three small children at home all under the age of three.

To make room for their growing family, the Fluders moved to a three-bedroom home surrounded by farmers' fields some twenty-five miles from Chicago. It was like living in the country. The sounds of cows mooing and tractors whirring woke them every morning. There was plenty of room to play outdoors in the fresh air. It was a great place to raise a family.

While none of the kids was difficult, Teri seemed to require almost no attention. She was quiet and always enjoyed playing by herself. Up until she was sixteen months old, she said almost nothing. Then one day she came up to Carol in the kitchen and uttered a complete sentence: "May I please have a drink of water?" Carol was astonished. She looked down at the little person standing next to her and wondered whether Teri had really spoken. Teri was never as verbal as her sisters. Rather than talk, she would sit and take everything in. She appeared, even as a toddler, to be an astute observer.

Three years later, the Fluder's only son, Paul, was born. Teri adjusted to her baby brother's arrival the same way she'd accepted Laura's birth—with no visible jealousy or trauma. She remained the easiest of the four children to take care of, spending hours playing alone. When Amy was born three years after Paul, Teri again appeared to take the birth of another sibling in stride.

The family, now numbering seven, spent much of its time together outdoors. They camped, swam, and rode horses. The television set was rarely on. Elaine remembers coming home from school one day in tears because she was the only child in her second-grade class who had never seen the TV show "Spiderman." She felt embarrassed and left out.

Unlike many fathers who were either not around or distant emotionally, Ernie spent as much time at home as he could. He and his father had never been close. He didn't want the same distance to separate him from his own children.

When Teri was eight, the Fluders moved to a larger, four-bedroom home about a mile away. Though the three oldest girls still attended the same grammar school, they now had to take the bus instead of walking. They lost that feeling of closeness with the other kids in their old neighborhood. The move was particularly hard on Teri. Her best friend had lived next door. Now it seemed as if she lived on another planet. Because Teri was quiet and shy, she had trouble making new friends. And often when she did, it seemed as if Laura stepped in and took the friend away. It was some time before Teri made friends with a girl across the street.

Because there weren't enough bedrooms to go around, Teri and Elaine doubled up. Though they had their share of sisterly disagreements, their love of books bound them together. Teri, especially, read all the time. She loved books that transported her to another place and time. *The Little House* series was one of her favorites. Even as a youngster, Teri thought nothing of staying up half the night to finish a book. Teri lost herself in books, escaping from the real world.

By the time she was nine, Teri had gained a lot of weight. Elaine remembers one day when she and Teri went ice skating at a local rink. Teri's plump body and short haircut made her look like a boy. When the rink manager announced that it was the girls' turn to skate, she and Elaine took to the ice. Just then a stranger turned to Teri and said, "Hey, this is the *girls'* time to skate." Elaine was horrified. She knew how crushed *she* felt and could only imagine what Teri was feeling. Teri grew up hating the way she looked, even when she lost weight and wore a size seven.

Though she didn't like the way she looked and had a tough time making friends, Teri wasn't a rebellious kid. She minded her own business at home, never making trouble. When it was time to go to sleep, she went straight to bed. She didn't challenge rules and regulations: They were meant to be followed. She avoided arguments at all costs. She wasn't a fighter. At school, too, she was well behaved. Until her junior year, she got good grades and was never in trouble. Her dream was to become an architect.

That all changed Teri's junior year. Her best friend had moved to Florida during the summer. The two had been inseparable. Now Teri had to make other friends. Her new friends were what Elaine called "The Freaks." Their top priority was having a good time. Studying took a backseat. Teri's grades dropped. But she was having fun. Friends called; there was always something to do. For the first time in her life, she was in the center of things, surrounded by a group of people who liked and accepted her. Teri's parents weren't thrilled with some of the friends or with the drop in grades. But they saw Teri's change in personality as a healthy one. She had finally come out of her shell. They knew she had the brains to excel academically whenever she wanted to.

Teri had taken drafting and art classes in high school. She enjoyed the work and the challenge. When she didn't sign up for any art at all junior year, her parents were surprised. She had seemed so interested. When they asked her why, Teri said she was "no good." Her art teacher from the year before had told her to forget about becoming an architect; she didn't have the talent. Teri took the criticism to heart. She didn't draw again for almost two years.

Senior year was a disaster. Teri started cutting classes and was suspended from school several times. She lost at least two part-time jobs for coming to work late. And she couldn't sleep. She'd lie awake all night, tossing and turning. Reading no longer calmed her down. One evening, after going out with friends and realizing it was too late to go home, she stayed in her parents' car all night. The angrier and more frustrated her parents got, the quieter Teri grew. She refused to talk about what might be bothering her. She said there was nothing wrong.

But there was a lot wrong. Teri had decided to run away. She couldn't take the pressure at home any longer. She jumped out of her second-floor bedroom window and took off. Luckily, one of her friends found her and talked her into going home. Her attempt to run away was the last straw. Her parents insisted that she get some help. After much coaxing, she agreed to talk to a parish priest who had a degree in counseling. After her first visit, she came home convinced that she didn't need to see him again. "Everything's fine," she told her parents. Under pressure, she did talk to the priest one more time. After that second visit, the priest told her parents that she was just going through normal teenage stress and that there was nothing to worry about. Both her parents were relieved. They trusted the priest's judgment and believed him when he said that Teri's problems would pass.

Although she hadn't shown any interest in school for over a year, Teri applied to the University of Illinois, where her father had gone. She was not accepted. Disappointed, she halfheartedly decided to go to Northern Illinois University in the fall. She spent the remainder of her senior year and the summer that followed partying and getting more and more depressed. She had the feeling no one liked her, not even her close friends. When a group of them threw her an eighteenth-birthday party, she came home in tears. She said everyone was making fun of her. She cried a lot and spent more and more time alone. Her mother was so distressed that she considered putting Teri into the hospital. Everyone told her that *she* was crazy.

Two days before Teri was to leave for college, her mother took her shopping for a dress to wear to a cousin's wedding. Teri hated everything she tried on. Nothing looked right.

"It makes me look fat," she said, standing in front of the mirror in one of the dresses.

"Teri," her mother said, "you weigh one hundred and nine pounds and wear a size seven. You're not fat."

"I'm ugly."

Her mother took her by the shoulders. "Look at yourself," she said, urging her to look at her reflection in the mirror. "Where are you ugly? What's ugly?"

"I'm just ugly," Teri said, staring past her reflection.

Her mother didn't know what to do. Here was her daughter, so unhappy, about to go away to college. Teri didn't have a close friend going to the same school; she would be on her own. Maybe she should stay home for a semester, go to a local junior college. When Teri's mother made the suggestion, Teri refused. "If you won't drive me to school, I'll get someone else to take me." Driving her wasn't the issue, her mother tried to explain. She was concerned about her. "Well, I'm going," Teri said. "That's all there is to it."

Her mother wasn't satisfied. She called her sister and a good friend. She needed their advice. What should she do? Both women told her she was overreacting. Teri would be fine. She was just nervous and excited. Leaving home for the first time was a trying experience. Teri would find a niche for herself soon enough. When Teri's mother went to work that night, she told several of her co-workers that college would either "make or break Teri."

LOOKING BACK . . . searching for answers, Carol and Ernie can only guess why Teri took her own life. They've gone over and over their last hours with her, trying desperately to find some clues.

Teri was very quiet during the drive to Northern, but that was understandable. She was scared. Who wouldn't be? Elaine had told them how she had cried for three days straight the year before. It wasn't surprising that Teri was nervous.

When they arrived at the dorm, Teri had to check in with a Resident Assistant. The young man made some flip comment about the Snoopy T-shirt she was wearing. He was trying to put her at ease, but Teri was noticeably upset. Then he gave her a short lecture about not losing her key and locking herself out of her room. He made a big deal out of it.

When she and her parents finally got to her room, they met Teri's roommate. She was around for a short time before leaving for home. Teri didn't seem to mind. She quietly started to unpack. Elaine showed up, surprising everyone, and Carol and Ernie said good-bye around 6:30 P.M.

"I'll call you as soon as I get my phone connected on Monday," Teri promised.

Her parents felt better.

"Don't worry," she said. "I can handle it. I'll be fine."

Around ten that night, after spending time with some of the girls across the hall, Teri discovered that she had locked herself out of her room. She had to go and find the Resident Assistant who had lectured her earlier in the day. He let her into her room and came back at 11:30 to make sure she was settled. When she didn't answer his knock, he assumed she was asleep. No one saw her again until her roommate opened the closet door late the next afternoon.

Teri didn't leave a suicide note. She had killed herself without any attempt to explain why.

FOUR YEARS AFTER Teri died, Elaine drove to DeKalb to read the autopsy report on her sister. She had thought about it for a long time, hoping beyond hope to find some explanation for what had happened. After four years of looking for answers, she still didn't understand why.

According to the report, Teri had first tried to slash her wrists with Bic razors. The police had found several of them in the wastepaper basket. That explained the mysterious marks on her wrists. But there was nothing else. No note. No other clues. Whatever her reasons, Teri had taken them with her. Elaine stopped grieving that day in the coroner's office; she stopped asking why. She knew there would never be any answers.

Carol isn't sure when she stopped asking why. It was a gradual process that took many years. But she now sees the first time she openly expressed her anger about Teri as a turning point. She and her youngest daughter, Amy, were on their way home from Amy's first counseling session. Amy was fourteen and having a hard time. Old friends of Teri's kept saying things like, "You remind us a lot of your sister." Amy was confused. If she reminded so many people of Teri, maybe she was like her. She cried all the way home.

Carol was furious. She went to the cemetery that afternoon . . . a place where she had done a lot of crying in the years since Teri had died. But this day was different; she was hopping mad. And she told Teri so. What right did she have to cause so much pain? What right did she have to ruin Amy's life, too? Getting angry felt good. And, though she felt a twinge of guilt, Carol's search for answers grew gradually less pressing.

Ernie doesn't know when he stopped working through his daughter's suicide. With time, his pain has been dulled, but never erased. It's something that will be with him for the rest of his life.

IN 1979, the Fluders, along with three other families and Father Charles Rubey of Catholic Charities in Chicago, started a support group called Loving Outreach to Survivors of Suicide (LOSS). Today, there are more than 350 people on the mailing list, and there are separate groups for parents, siblings, and spouses. Members of LOSS say that the chance to talk about their feelings indefinitely with others who have suffered similar losses helps them deal with their grief. No one can tell how long the grieving process will take. It is different for everyone. LOSS understands this and lets its members participate for as long as they need to.

There are support groups like LOSS in most major cities across the country. If you or someone you know would like more information about the suicide survivors' support groups in your area, try looking in the white pages under *Contact* or *Samaritans.* Both groups should have listings of support groups. You might also call the American Association of Suicidology during business hours at 303-692-0985.

# ( 4 )

# *Exploding the Myths/*
# *Recognizing*
# *the Warning Signals*

I F TERI FLUDER'S family had known then what they know now, chances are good that they could have prevented Teri's death. But the Fluders had never known anyone who had died by suicide. They didn't know what distress signals to watch for or what they could have done. They trusted the priest who pronounced Teri to be a typical teenager whose problems would pass with time.

Tragically, the Fluders are not alone. They, like the families of the thousands of other teens who kill themselves each year, missed the warning signals. They hadn't been educated to watch for them.

EVEN THE EXPERTS don't know why Teri and more than five thousand American teenagers take their own lives every year. What they *do* know is that they *and* you can help. For every one teenager who kills him- or herself, there may be as many as one hundred others who try and fail. This fact offers hope. Most teens who attempt suicide don't really want to die or are prevented from succeeding.

### "STOP ME, PLEASE"

1. Seventy-five percent of suicide attempters give repeated warnings. They tell their friends, sometimes even their families, that they want to die. They are asking for help.
2. Nine out of ten teenagers who attempt suicide do so in the home, where there is a good chance that someone will stop them.
3. In the few months before taking their own lives, seventy-five percent of the victims had seen their family doctor. Many of them were also seeing a psychiatrist.

### HOPE

The facts tell the story. Most teens who attempt suicide want to be seen, stopped, and saved. They want to live. It's a myth that once a teen decides to take his or her own life that there is nothing anyone can do to stop him or her. The truth is that there is plenty that can be done. Friends like you can make the difference. It's only when you believe the myths about suicide that it is hard to act.

EXPLODING THE SUICIDE MYTHS

Test yourself. Are the following statements true or false?

1. Joe and Jeff told a group of their friends that they were going to kill themselves by "flying off a cliff." Because they talked about killing themselves in front of friends, they were just looking for attention and wouldn't actually go ahead with their plan.

2. Once Ron made up his mind to kill himself and said good-bye to his friends, nothing anyone could do could stop him.

3. Jeffrey tried to kill himself by swallowing thirty-five aspirin tablets. He got sick and had a ringing in his ears for four days. After the discomfort and fright he felt, Jeffrey probably won't attempt suicide again.

4. Steve's depression seemed to have lifted. All of his problems appeared to be behind him. He was back in school and studying hard. He was out of danger.

5. Anna, Janie's best friend, knew Janie was depressed and thinking about suicide. But Anna also knew that talking to Janie about suicide would only give her ideas and make things worse.

6. People who kill themselves are crazy.

MYTH: *When people talk about killing themselves, they're just looking for attention. Ignoring them is the best thing to do.*

REALITY: *The truth is that most teens who take their own lives do talk about it. Eighty percent of adolescent suicides make open threats before they kill themselves.*

Joe and Jeff, both sixteen, had been best friends since sixth grade. Back then, Joe had needed a buddy badly. His parents had argued constantly ever since he could remember and had finally separated when Joe was in fourth grade. That's when he started talking back to his teachers and picking fights. By sixth grade he'd become a loan shark, loaning money to his classmates and doubling the debt if they didn't pay him back the next day. Jeff looked up to Joe as a "real cool operator."

In seventh grade, Joe started drinking and smoking pot. He'd go to school stoned and would fall into bed at 6:30 every night. His mother didn't seem to notice. One month before Joe turned thirteen, his mother remarried. Eight months later, she left the house and joined her new husband in another city, 120 miles away. Joe's life came undone.

Joe's father returned to raise him and his two brothers; things went from bad to worse. As far as Joe was concerned, his father cut him down every chance he got. Nothing he did or said was right. Joe hated his life at home and started spending as much time as he could with Jeff and Jeff's family.

After their cattle ranch ran into hard times, Jeff's family moved into town. Jeff's mother got a job as a police dispatcher; his father sold cars. And then *their* life started to go wrong. Jeff's father worked long hours and drank heavily. He had little time left for his family. Then he got involved with another woman. Jeff's parents separated, then got back together. But things were never the same.

Jeff's behavior at home started to change. He became withdrawn and started smoking pot and drinking. Both he and Joe were increasingly unhappy. They fought with their fathers and saw the little town where they lived as a prison where nothing would ever change.

The first time they talked about suicide, the boys fantasized about going to Pole Creek where they'd swallow some sleeping pills and lie down on the grass to die. But they weren't really serious . . . not then.

The two friends talked about suicide again, only this time there was a new plan: They could drive off the cliff at Dead Man's Curve. The boys still hadn't set a date, but both agreed that killing themselves that way would probably be painless.

One Monday morning, Jeff and Joe skipped school. They got drunk, talked, and drove around town. Maybe this was the day to try out Dead Man's Curve, they thought. Close to dinnertime, they picked up a friend and drove her around. Jeff told her they were going to fly through the air off a cliff. He also said they would come back alive. The friend didn't believe him. On their way to the high school, Joe stepped on the accelerator, hit ninety, lost control of the car, hit a fence, and spun off the road into the ditch. No one was hurt.

Later at the town library, standing around with a group of kids, Joe turned to Jeff and said, "Let's go kill ourselves."

"Yeah," Jeff said. "Let's go."

The others laughed.

"We're serious," Joe said. "We're going to fly off the cliff," he said as he and Jeff got into Joe's car.

One of the boys who had heard all of this tried to push his way into the car.

"Stop it," Joe said. "We don't want to be responsible for your death."

"Screw you," the boy said. He still didn't believe they were serious.

Jeff and Joe got out of the car one more time. They shook hands all around.

"I'll bring flowers to your grave," one of the girls said, laughing.

Joe took off a cap he was wearing and gave it to another girl. "You'll never see me again. Keep it for memories."

Still, no one thought they were serious.

"You don't believe us," Joe said, "but we're going to do it. You can read about it in the paper tomorrow."

WHEN HE REGAINED consciousness, Joe saw paramedics kneeling over him. "What happened to my friend?" he asked. "What happened to Jeff?"

Three days later, Jeff was buried. The grave was marked by a simple stone that read:

Loved Son and Brother
Jeffrey Scott Allen Westerberg
July 7, 1964–November 17, 1980
Gone Fishing

Joe and Jeff, like 75 percent of the teenagers who kill themselves, told their friends about their plan. Unfortunately, no one believed them.

*MYTH:   Once a person has decided to kill him-or herself, no one can stop him or her.*
*REALITY:   For almost all teenagers, suicide is a cry for help, not a wish to die. Even the most hopelessly suicidal person has mixed feelings about death, moving back and forth between wanting to*

*die and wanting to live. With help, even that person can be*
*stopped and pushed toward life.*

LIKE 90 PERCENT of young suicide attempters, Ron Neal
was probably hoping that his friends would rescue him
at the last minute. Otherwise, his parents ask, why did
he leave every door in the house unlocked? Why had
the automatic garage-door opener been unlatched, so
that the door could be opened by hand from the outside? And why was the door between the garage door
and the house kept open by a dog cage with a barking
dog inside?

Unfortunately for Ron, his friends arrived too late.
As they drove up the driveway, they saw the garage lights
on and heard a car running. They rushed to the garage
where they found Ron's limp body slumped behind the
wheel. He was already dead.

IN FRANCINE Klagsbrun's book *Too Young to Die,* the author
wrote about a young woman who spent weeks planning
her suicide. She jumped from her seventh-floor apartment
window, but a tree broke her fall. She survived. Later, she
talked about her feelings as she jumped. "As I began to
fall, I wanted more than anything to be able to turn back,
grab hold of the window ledge, and pull myself up."

TIM WAS FIFTEEN when he decided that life just wasn't
worth the hassle. He'd gotten into a fight at school earlier
in the day. The night before, he and his girl friend had had
a big argument. His friends were mad at him, too, and he
didn't know why.

"I was just really mixed up . . . I was making the

people around me miserable, too, so I thought the best thing for me to do was kill myself."

Tim had made a noose and put it in his bedroom. He thought it looked really cool. No one thought that he was serious about using it.

Tim was saved by his older brother, who came home unexpectedly in the middle of the day, broke into the house through the back window, and cut his brother down. When the paramedics arrived, Tim was unconscious.

"I guess I'm pretty damn lucky," he says now. "Being in the hospital kind of cleared my head. Before, I'd walk around either so stoned or so confused that I didn't know what I was doing a lot of the time. It made me learn to take things much easier."

On the second anniversary of Tim's suicide attempt, his friends gave him a party.

"I'm glad my brother came home early that afternoon."

MYTH: *Once a person tries to kill him-or herself and fails, the pain and shame will keep him or her from trying again.*

REALITY: *Of every five people who take their own lives, four have made one or more previous attempts. And of all teenagers who attempt suicide, one in three tries again.*

JEFFREY had thought about suicide every day for six months. He hated who he was—"just ordinary." He didn't get the praise he needed from his parents and felt that they paid more attention to his brothers and sisters.

The first time he attempted suicide, Jeffrey waited until his family had left for the day. Then he swallowed thirty-five aspirin tablets, one by one. He drank a beer and lay down to die. Then he started to get really sick. His ears rang for four days. He told some friends about what he'd done. They didn't seem to believe him.

Six weeks later, Jeffrey decided to try again. He drank Jack Daniels until he got up the courage to use the handgun he had put on top of his bedroom dresser. But he was too drunk to get up. Instead, he passed out.

Luckily, Jeffrey didn't get a chance to try a third time. Before that could happen, a friend read a journal he was keeping for one of his classes. It was filled with thoughts of death. The friend told the school social worker, who met first with Jeffrey, then with his parents. Jeffrey was rushed to a psychiatrist, who insisted he be hospitalized immediately. Jeffrey spent the next four months in the hospital, where he gained a new lease on life. If his friend hadn't stepped in, chances are that Jeffrey wouldn't be around today. His advice to other suicidal teens: "Don't do it."

MYTH:   *When a suicidal person's depression appears to have lifted and s/he's acting so much better and happier, s/he's out of danger.*

REALITY:   *Depression can be most dangerous just when it appears to be lifting. When a person is severely depressed, s/he may want to die but may lack the energy and power to carry out a plan. But when she feels a bit better, it's easier to carry through with a suicide.*

THE PSYCHIATRIST who saw Steve wrote a letter to the marine recruiting office saying that he was severely depressed. He had stopped eating. He couldn't sleep. And he had threatened to cut off his big toe.

After Steve got out of entering the marines, the depression seemed to lift. He started classes at a junior college, got a part-time job, and made plans to take out a girl he liked.

Three months later, he was dead. He shot himself in the head with a .22 caliber gun.

WHEN a fifteen-year-old suburban Chicago boy killed himself, his family was shocked. "Things seemed to be going so much better for him. He appeared to have adjusted to our move to a new school district. And he had made plans to go fishing."

*MYTH:   Talking to a troubled person about suicide will just give him/her ideas.*

*REALITY:   Another common mistake. You don't give a suicidal person ideas about suicide. The ideas are already there. Talking about them honestly and openly will help, not hurt. Most troubled people really want to talk about what's bothering them. It's a relief to get their pain out into the open, as long as they know their feelings will be taken seriously and with understanding. One of the biggest mistakes people make when talking to a troubled teen is to deny the teen's problems or to tell him or her that the problems aren't really serious and will pass.*

*MYTH:   People who kill themselves are crazy.*

*REALITY:   Most suicidal people are not insane. Although many of those who try to kill themselves feel depressed, lonely, and hopeless, they are not mentally ill. This fact offers great hope. With the right treatment, someone who is depressed has an 80 to 90 percent chance for a full recovery.*

Now that you understand the many myths surrounding suicide, how can you catch a friend before he/she attempts suicide? What signs can you look for?

### SOS SUICIDE: WARNING SIGNALS

Cathy was the older of two children. She was a homecoming queen, cheerleader, and popular *B* student who had been accepted at college. After an argument with her longtime boyfriend, she went into her bathroom and hanged herself.

Cathy's family and friends were stunned. Nobody had had any idea that there had been something wrong. Cathy had had everything going for her. She'd been the perfect teenager. Or so everyone had thought.

Looking back, Cathy's family was able to see some of the problems that may have led to her suicide. But the signs of her unhappiness were unclear at the time and went unnoticed. Only after her death were the distress signals more apparent. Only then did Cathy's family and friends realize that she had felt tremendous pressure to be "perfect" and that she almost never had talked to anyone about her own feelings and problems.

Does that mean that you can never tell whether a friend is suicidal? Absolutely not. There *are* warning signals—some clearer than others—that indicate something is wrong. What's important is that you understand these warning signals and use them as a barometer for trouble.

### SIX GENERAL WARNING SIGNALS

The following six warning signals reflect that there is trouble. While they don't mean that someone you know is on the verge of suicide, they do indicate that something is wrong.

### 1. Acting Out: Aggressive, Hostile Behavior

If you or your friends have problems, what do you do to blow off steam? Drink? Use drugs? Drive like maniacs? A lot of teens who feel angry and unhappy do those things. Some go a step further and get into fights, shoplift, or even run away from home. Acting out—behavior that thumbs its nose at rules and authority—often means that something is wrong.

### 2. Alcohol and Drug Abuse

Almost half the teenagers who commit suicide are drunk or high shortly before their deaths. And 85 percent of teenage attempters had too much to drink or were high on drugs.

If you or your friends drink or use drugs, think about the times someone overdid it. Maybe s/he was trying to drown some sorrow—bad grades, breakup with a boyfriend or girl friend, or hard times at home.

If you and your friends don't use drugs or alcohol, you probably know people who do. Are they just out for a good time, or are they covering up for their insecurities or problems?

Drugs and alcohol often make a depressed person even more depressed. And they cause people to act without thinking clearly.

### 3. Passive Behavior

Have you ever felt that you just can't get moving, that it's too hard to do anything, and that there's not much worth doing, anyway? That's passive behavior, and many depressed/suicidal teens feel that way most of the time. "It's like being wrapped in Saran Wrap, trying to get through but never making it past the plastic," said one suicide attempter. Kate, another attempter, described her passivity as feeling nothing, having to burn herself with an iron just to know that she was alive.

Passive teens are afraid to let their anger and frustrations show. If they did, they might get carried away: All the rage they've been keeping inside might fester and explode.

### 4. Changes in Eating Habits

Mary grew up feeling that she wasn't as good as everyone else around her. She set very high standards for herself and never thought she measured up. Her home life didn't do much to make her feel any better. Her parents always seemed on the verge of divorce. By the end of eighth grade, her parents separated, and Mary, a chunky 135 pounds, almost stopped eating. "It seemed like everybody hated me, and it was kind of like my way of getting my parents back together and getting back at people who make fun of me and to scare them." She lost 47 pounds over the next year, shrinking down to a mere 88 pounds.

While most suicidal teens don't become anorexic like Mary, they may change their eating habits dramatically. Healthy eaters may start nibbling at their food or not eating at all, while picky eaters may start eating as if there's no tomorrow.

### 5. Changes in Sleeping Habits

As you remember, in the months before nineteen-year-old Teri Fluder killed herself, she stopped sleeping. The books that used to calm her down and eventually put her to sleep didn't help anymore. Because of her lack of sleep, Teri was tired all the time and started showing up late to her part-time job. She eventually lost that job and a second one because of tardiness.

On the other hand, someone who may have slept normally or too little may start sleeping too much. After Mark shot himself to death, his parents tried to uncover what unrecognized signals he might have given. Mark's father remembered: "During the last week he seemed to be sleeping more. He'd go to bed early and then he'd get up late and go off to school, so that we never really had a chance to talk to him."

### 6. Fear of Separation

Do you remember how you felt the first day in kindergarten or your first night away from home? Leaving your parents and home can be difficult. But for someone who is troubled, such separation can be traumatic. If a friend suddenly seems uncomfortable about sleeping over or having his/her parents go away, it may mean trouble is brewing.

#### SPECIFIC SUICIDE WARNING SIGNALS

The first group of six warning signals set the stage for trouble. The next six indicate a loss of control and balance. The troubled teenager can no longer hide the pain.

### 7. Abrupt Changes in Personality

You remember that Teri Fluder had always been quiet and shy. She had trouble making friends and, from the time she was a toddler, seemed content to play by herself. When she turned sixteen, her personality changed abruptly. She started hanging out with a wilder group of kids, whose main goal in life was to have a good time. The phone rang all the time. Teri always had something to do and friends to be with. Once a good student, she now stopped studying. Teri's parents weren't happy about the drop in grades but felt that she'd finally come out of her shell. Less than two years later, she was dead.

Sudden changes in personality can be a sign that a friend has become preoccupied with suicide. The problem is that most teens aren't settled about themselves and their place in the world, and changes in personality occur often, even in those who are not depressed. The key is whether the changes are different from the usual pattern.

Amy had been an outgoing, happy fifteen-year-old who had many friends and participated in a lot of school activities. Suddenly, she started spending more and more time by herself. She stopped all of her outside activities, choosing instead to sit alone in her room for hours at a time. She attempted suicide by slitting her wrists.

*8. Sudden Mood Swings*

Who hasn't had days when they feel great one minute and down the next? Moodiness is part of being a teenager. But if these sudden mood swings continue for long periods, they're *not* normal.

Melissa was somber and withdrawn. She stopped spending time with her friends, choosing instead to spend all of her free time alone in her bedroom with the door locked. Then, one evening, she got dressed and went to a friend's party. She danced, sang, and talked a blue streak. She was the "life of the party." But the next day, just as suddenly as her mood had seemed to improve, she was back in the dumps, refusing once again even to talk to her friends.

### 9. Risky Behavior

Ted flirted with death several times before actually killing himself with carbon-monoxide poisoning in his parents' garage. One of his friends remembers the afternoon after an ROTC parade when Ted got behind the wheel of his car and started driving like a maniac. He pulled out right in front of a huge truck, scaring his friend half to death. When Ted got back to school and parked his car, he turned to his rattled friend and said, "Somebody could really die in a car." His risky behavior could have alerted his friend that Ted was ready to take big chances with his life and those of others. But it's easy to overlook such boasting and talking big, because such behavior is part of trying on adolescence.

### 10. Decreased Interest in School and Poor Grades

Because school is a major part of your life, it is also one of the best measures of your and your friends' mental health. If a friend's grades fall dramatically, the chances are good that something is wrong. Dale was an excellent student. Studying came easily for him. He got $A$'s all through junior high school. But when he started high school, he seemed to lose interest in his schoolwork. He'd drift off or read a book instead. His grades fell to mostly $D$'s. Dale made his first suicide attempt toward the end of his freshman year.

### 11. Inability to Concentrate

When a friend can't concentrate long enough to read a short magazine article or review homework for a test, it is most likely because s/he is absorbed in her/his own inner turmoil.

Sid had been an outstanding student all through high school. Suddenly, his grades started to fall. He couldn't concentrate long enough to finish reading a paragraph. Luckily, his parents noticed the problem early on and got Sid professional help.

### 12. Loss or Lack of Friends

Many teens who end up suicidal never had friends to lose. Justin was one of those kids. He never fit in very well. He was very critical of kids his own age and often cut them down. He would rather read science fiction or listen to Beethoven than do the "common" things everybody else was doing. Justin hanged himself on Valentine's Day, maybe because, as his mother explained, he felt that everyone else in the world was in love or had somebody except him.

Several studies have found that many teenagers who took their own lives didn't have or didn't feel that they had a close friend. There wasn't one special person to whom they could turn and who accepted them and their feelings.

If someone you know seems unhappy, be a good friend. Don't argue about why he/she should be happy, and don't tell him/her things like, "You can't possibly feel as bad as you say." Listen and go for help if you think your friend might be suicidal. Tell an adult, preferably a teacher, counselor, or psychologist. (More about this in Chapter 7.)

FINAL DISTRESS SIGNALS: IMPENDING DOOM

*13. Loss of an Important Person or Thing*

For a teenager who is already troubled and unable to hide the pain, death, divorce, or breakup with a boyfriend or girl friend can be the last straw.

Natalie had always thought about suicide. Her mother was mentally ill and her father was a strict disciplinarian who had trouble showing love and support. But Natalie had joined a street gang and found, at least temporarily, a substitute family. School wasn't going well, but Natalie had a boyfriend. That was all that mattered. When he broke up with her, her world collapsed. She made her first suicide attempt soon after the breakup.

Charles was the younger of two children. "He was the happiest little boy you ever saw," his mother said. He loved music and could play the cello before he could read. When Charles was eight, his father had a serious heart attack. And that's when Charles stopped being happy. Though his father eventually recovered, Charles blamed himself for his father's illness. As he grew older, he became withdrawn and more and more depressed. He died by strangulation in his family's shower.

*14. Hopelessness*

Jeffrey was a very active kid. But suddenly everything got to be too much for him. He quit his part-time job at a pizza place. He stopped doing his homework. And he dropped a new girl friend because she'd only be "another burden." Life appeared hopeless, and Jeffrey decided he was more trouble than he was worth.

Nothing makes a hopeless teenager happy—not food, friends, activities, or accomplishments. "I might as well be dead," wrote one teen in a suicide note.

### *15. Obsession with Death*

Vivienne Loomis had been obsessed with death long before she walked into her mother's studio, tied a rope around her neck, and hanged herself. Life had come to contain too much pain. For Vivienne, death meant an end to that pain. She wrote about death constantly: "Death is going to be a beautiful thing." And she talked about death with a friend. "I knew from what she told me that she was very, very serious about suicide. . . . Sometimes she'd tell me that she'd tried to strangle herself." Vivienne rehearsed her suicide many times. She worked to overcome her fear of it by experimenting with fainting and strangulation. By the time she actually hanged herself, death had lost its horror.

### *16. Making a Will/Giving Away Possessions*

Before Mary attempted suicide for the third time, she gave pictures of herself to friends so that they would have something to remember her by.

Before Jeff tried to kill himself, he wrote a "will," leaving his record collection to a friend and his sports equipment to his younger brother.

Teenagers who are getting ready to die often give away some of their possessions to a sibling or a friend. They are, in a sense, executing their own wills. Making a will is perhaps the most serious sign of a potential suicide.

WHAT CAN YOU DO?

Teens who are thinking seriously about suicide will need professional help to work out their problems. But, as a friend, you can:

1. Recognize the warning signals
2. Trust your own judgment and take action if you suspect real danger (never leave a suicidal friend alone)
3. Listen intelligently
4. Be supportive
5. Urge professional help
6. Tell a parent, teacher, or counselor

*NEVER KEEP A FRIEND'S SUICIDAL FEELINGS A SECRET.*

# (5)

# They Say "Time Heals All Wounds": His Parents' Story

"Time heals all wounds," they say. "Life goes on," they add. Cold comfort for a mother whose son has just killed himself—who is in a state of shock—living in a nightmare. A mother filled with unanswered questions and self-doubts who prays for strength to survive this ordeal— to keep her husband and children from falling into an abyss of unbearable grief and guilt. A mother who is screaming and sobbing wildly inside, but who cannot shed a tear. A mother tormented by the anguish of her son's pain, which she was unable to stop.

After four years, the nightmares still occur, but not as often. A calm has settled over all. Her husband and

*children have gone on with their lives. The self-doubts have
all but disappeared. The tears flow easily when touched by
memories.*

*No, time does not heal all wounds. Time softens pain;
time dulls grief. Questions remain unanswered.*

*Yes, life does go on and life is good. It is lived with
the memory of a dearly beloved son.*

Shirley Mersky

*1982—four years after her son's suicide*

**H**AVE YOU EVER thought how parents must feel when a child of theirs takes his or her own life? The tremendous guilt? The endless searching for answers? The overwhelming sense of loss? One father whose fourteen-year-old daughter killed herself said that he knew what it was to feel "just utterly damned." Is suicide worth getting back at parents?

Maybe the parents of some teenage suicide victims hadn't always done the best job. Sometimes they may have made it hard to talk about anything. One nineteen-year-old who tried to kill herself twice said, "My parents have certain values and beliefs, and I didn't feel they would like me if I went and told them how I felt about things. They would really hate my guts and wouldn't want me as a daughter."

The way your parents treat you has a lot to do with how you feel about yourself and how you handle your problems. Parents who back you up—who accept you for who you are—can be a big help. Parents who think that only *they* know what is good for you can make it rough.

Maybe you're one of the lucky ones who can talk about almost anything with both of your parents. Or maybe you can talk to one of your parents but not to the other. Whatever your situation at home, one thing is certain: Most parents do the best job they know how.

————

BEV AND RON GESKE couldn't wait to start a family. They weren't trained to be parents. They just jumped in and learned by trial and error. This is their story.

RON GESKE and a buddy of his went to a local hospital dance, just outside of Chicago, one Saturday night back in 1956. Within a few minutes after arriving at the dance, Ron got lucky. He spotted a petite blonde and got up the nerve to ask her to dance. By the end of the night, Ron had asked Bev Birmingham out on a date.

Bev's dream ever since she was in high school was to be a nurse. Ron never thought of continuing his formal education after high school. His father was a machinist, and, ever since he could remember, Ron had wanted to be a machinist, too.

Ron and Bev were married just two weeks before Ron began his stint with the U.S. Army, where he was stationed outside of Boston. Bev stayed behind in Chicago to finish her nursing degree. But the newlyweds saw each other whenever they could during the four months they lived apart. And as soon as Bev graduated, she joined Ron on the army base. She was three months pregnant.

Bev wanted a son. She had the name Steve picked out from the beginning. Ron didn't care much whether he had a boy or a girl, as long as the baby was healthy.

Patricia was born in the army hospital in January. Her sister, Susan, was born in the same hospital ten months later. Christine, the third girl, arrived in January of 1962. And a year and three days later, Steve, the boy Bev had always wanted, was born. The Geskes had had four children in less than four years!

By the time Steve was born, Ron was out of the army. The family of six had moved into a modest suburban home. Ron worked rotating shifts as a machinist; Bev stayed home with the four kids. Life was extremely hectic, but fun. Ron's sisters and sisters-in-law were all having children at the same time, so the Geske kids and their many cousins grew up together. They played often and spent every holiday at Ron's folks. Theirs was one large, extended family.

When they were young, all four of Ron and Bev's children got along well. The girls, particularly Susan, were good to their baby brother. Susan played with Steve, read to him, taught him his numbers and colors. Because she and Steve looked so much alike—the same size and reddish hair—they were sometimes mistaken for twins.

Once in school, there was no mistaking Steve and Susan for twins. They weren't anything alike. Susan and her older sister, Patricia, were outstanding students— bright, responsive, and hard-working. Both girls set high standards and never disappointed themselves or anyone else.

Steve, on the other hand, never seemed to know what he wanted to do. He didn't show any real interest in working with his hands, as Ron had hoped he would. And he didn't excel in any subjects at school. He did like scouting, though, and played Little League baseball for a couple of years. He was a good player but seemed to shy away from competition. It was as if he didn't want to be disappointed in himself or let others down.

Ron had hoped that his son and he would have more

in common. He took Steve fishing, but Steve wasn't that interested. He took him down to the local fire station where he was a volunteer fireman, but Steve didn't show much enthusiasm. (Years later, however, Steve enrolled in a two-year fire science program at a junior college.) Steve wasn't much for talking. When something was very important, he would talk with his father. Otherwise, he kept his feelings to himself.

Around the time he turned twelve, Steve started having trouble in school. The junior-high principal called his parents several times. Steve was pushing kids in the lunch line and fighting with other boys. When Bev asked Steve what was going on, he said a big kid was pushing some other little kid and that he had stepped in. Bev passed that story on to the principal, hoping he would see Steve's side of the story. He didn't. Kids weren't supposed to fight in school. Period.

Steve's grades started falling. He was always looking for an excuse not to go to school. By the time he started high school, he had a truancy problem. Bev was worried. She was spending what seemed like her whole life on the phone calling in and making excuses for Steve. After each call, she vowed not to lie for him again. But she just couldn't stand letting him suffer the consequences of his truancy. So she'd give in and call every time he skipped school. To this day, she wonders whether she made a mistake by covering up for Steve so often.

Ron didn't go for excuses. As far as he was concerned, every kid was supposed to know what he was doing with his life by the time he was fifteen or sixteen. Either you got a trade after high school or you went to college. For a while, Steve talked about driving a truck. But he changed his mind. He didn't feel like doing that or anything else. Ron was furious. He took out his anger by yelling. Steve hated the yelling. He felt like hitting his dad sometimes, but he never did. He punched holes in his bedroom wall instead. His wall looked like a big hunk of Swiss cheese.

Ron says he worried that something wasn't quite right with Steve, but never thought about getting professional help. Steve was a loner. He spent hours by himself in his room. Ron didn't like that; it bothered him that Steve couldn't make or didn't want friends. But Steve liked his privacy and used his time alone to good advantage. He collected coins and could tell you where each coin came from and how much it was worth. He was a trivia buff, too, and read things like *The Book of Lists* and *The People's Almanac* from cover to cover. When he was sixteen, Steve asked his parents for a Bible. Steve's apparent interest in God and religion was a good sign. Ron went out and bought Steve a Bible.

If Steve had found religion, he kept it to himself. But his near obsession with physical fitness was common knowledge. On school nights, he went to bed around nine. That way, he could get up early enough the next morning to work out before school. His parents usually awoke to the sounds of weights clanging and Steve grunting. Steve was a well-built kid who responded to the personal challenge of making his body even stronger. Still, he shied away from attention. When physical fitness tests were held in school, he would stand on the sidelines as everyone else cheered on the school jock to do still another push-up. Then he'd lie down on the gym floor and do more push-ups than two of the jocks combined. Quietly, he'd finish his set, get up, and walk away.

Steve was quiet about his accomplishments in tae

kwon do, too. Within a year and a half, he had worked all the way up to a black belt. His room was covered with ribbons he'd won in martial arts competitions. Yet neither his parents nor his friends had ever set foot inside the tae kwon do school to watch him practice or compete.

In order to pay for the martial arts classes and to have money of his own, Steve worked a variety of part-time jobs all through high school. He was an usher at a local theater. He delivered papers. And he worked at a 7-Eleven store. Much to his parents' chagrin, he never stuck with one job very long. Just when it seemed that he had a good thing going, he would quit. With all his moving from job to job, Steve still managed to save enough money to buy a 1971 Chevy sometime after his sixteenth birthday. That car was his pride and joy. He was always washing or polishing or doing something to it. He loved that car. No one—not even his sister, Chris, who helped herself to everything else—could have it. It was his.

When his sister Sue left home for college, Steve lost an ally and a friend. He had looked up to his sister and relied on her opinions and her support. Even though Sue and Steve didn't share the same friends in high school, they had remained close. Steve didn't say much after Sue left home, but he must have missed her a lot. The two only saw each other during the summer but they talked often on the phone. Sue kept asking Steve to send her a picture of himself.

With Sue and Patricia off at college, Steve was left at home with Chris. The two of them hadn't gotten along for years. Without Steve's other two sisters around to act as buffers, the feud between Steve and Chris mushroomed. Steve resented her going into his room without permission and helping herself to anything she could get her hands on. He couldn't stand the mess Chris left in her room and around the rest of the house. He hated her constant arguing with their parents. Things got so bad that Steve went out and bought a lock for his bedroom door. If he couldn't keep her out of the house, he could at least keep her out of his room.

Steve didn't have many friends . . . two guys across the street and a guy named Jeff. He didn't date, either. If he went out at all, he went with a group of kids. Maybe they'd go to a party or maybe they'd drive up to Wisconsin where the drinking age was eighteen. Steve looked a lot older than he was. He got served without any problem. His father knew about the Wisconsin drinking trips but wasn't bothered. He'd done the same thing when he was a teenager.

Steve drank beer but not hard stuff—at least as far as his parents could tell. He never came home reeking of alcohol or acting weird or out of control. He didn't cause problems the way Chris did. He was always home by midnight, and his few friends seemed like good kids who stayed out of trouble.

That was more than anyone could say about Chris's friends. She was running around with a group of "undesirables"—staying out all night, getting into trouble. Chris was having a hard time and making life miserable for her parents and for Steve.

Everything came to a head during Steve's senior year. Chris backed down the driveway without looking and crashed into Steve's beloved Chevy. As far as Chris was concerned, Steve shouldn't have parked his car there. Still, she knew she had better get the heck out of the house before Steve got home. When Steve arrived home later that day, he was heartbroken. He had had his car for less than a year and loved it more than anything else in the world. It was a good thing Chris wasn't around. Steve might have killed her.

In January of his senior year, Steve turned eighteen and signed up to join the marines as soon as he finished high school. Ron wasn't against his enlisting. He just didn't like the recruiters coming into the schools and "brainwashing" the kids to sign up. He felt they and all their fast talk were worse than used-car salesmen. Ron told Steve that if he was going to join the marines, he should sign up for something worthwhile that he could use later on.

Steve spent a lot of time in the next two or three months trying to interest other guys in enlisting. He had been promised a PFC status, one step above a private, if he could find two people who actually signed up. He talked up the marines and eventually got two guys to enlist. When he was told that one of the two had been recruited earlier by someone else, he was furious. He knew that he had been taken. The marines had no intention of making him a PFC.

By June of his senior year, Steve announced to his parents that he wasn't going into the marines. Ron was flabbergasted. What did he mean he didn't want to go? He had signed up. Steve said he had changed his mind. He didn't explain. His only concern now was how to get out. He talked to people and discovered that if he were accepted by a college, the marines would let him go. Steve quickly applied to a local two-year college and got in. He was relieved, certain that he'd beaten the marines at their own game. But when he showed his acceptance papers to the recruiting officer, his request was denied. The rules said he had to attend a four-year college.

It was now the end of June, and Steve had to try to weasel his way into a four-year school—not an easy task at such a late date with his mediocre grades. To add to the confusion, Chris had decided to move into a place of her own. Steve was too worried about getting out of the marines to enjoy his sister's move.

Steve applied to the University of Illinois/Chicago and was accepted. Armed with his second set of acceptance papers, he went back to the recruiting officer, who continued to give him a hard time. Steve was a mess. The marines had him trapped. There was no way out. That made him crazy. He stopped eating. He couldn't sleep. He told his parents that he was on the edge of a nervous breakdown.

Then he figured his way out. He would cut off his little toe. The marines wouldn't want him then. When his mother heard about the toe, she was shocked. Here was a guy, who had taken such special care of his body, talking about cutting off his toe. Steve had never even taken an aspirin, and now he was seriously thinking of maiming himself. His parents were frantic. They tried to explain how the little toe is the key to balance. They discussed the many problems Steve would face the rest of his life without it. Steve finally gave them his word: He wouldn't cut off his toe. But something had to be done; he had to get out of the marines.

Desperate, Steve found out that if he got a letter from a doctor saying that he was in no mental condition to join the marines, the marines would let him out. Bev worked in a medical clinic and made an appointment for Steve to see one of the doctors. The physician examined Steve and agreed that he was showing signs of a nervous breakdown. The doctor said that he would be happy to write a letter but felt it would sound more convincing coming from a psychiatrist. Bev agreed and hurriedly scheduled an appointment with one of the psychiatrists at the clinic. The pressure was unbearable. It was only a matter of weeks before Steve was supposed to start basic training.

Steve talked to the psychiatrist. A week later, he had the letter. It said that he was in a severe state of depression. The psychiatrist did not recommend treatment. That surprised Bev, but she figured once Steve had the mess with the marines settled, everything would return to normal. To be safe, Bev made several copies of the psychiatrist's letter. She had this awful feeling that she would never see Steve again. The marines were going to kidnap him and keep him forever.

The letter worked. Steve got out of the marines in late August and decided to attend the local two-year college where he had been accepted in June. He signed up for the fire science program and loved it. He came home, did his homework, and talked about his psychology class with his mother. Steve also worked two or three evenings a week as a security guard at a store in a large shopping center. He would take his books and sit in the back room of the store and study. Bev and Ron couldn't believe the turnaround. Steve seemed to have forgotten all about the trauma with the marines. He was calm, happy, and excited about college. The signs of "severe depression" had miraculously disappeared.

Late that autumn, Chris decided to move back home. She wasn't making enough money at the beauty shop where she was working to pay her rent. Her decision threw the rest of the family into real turmoil. It had been so peaceful and quiet without her. But what could Ron do? Kick his own daughter into the street? For him, it was a moral issue. He had had nothing but problems with Chris but couldn't refuse to give her a place to stay. Steve was furious. He couldn't understand why his parents would take Chris back. Hadn't they had enough of her flak? Steve told them he "would do something" if she moved back home.

Two weeks before Thanksgiving, Chris moved back in. Big garbage bags, boxes, and suitcases filled with her belongings piled up in the middle of the family room. She took her time unpacking. Steve ignored her. He was busy making plans for a big date that Saturday night with a girl from school. He wanted to take her to a nice restaurant and asked Bev for suggestions. They decided on a steak house.

The phone rang at two o'clock Sunday morning. It was a police officer calling to say that Steve had been picked up for speeding, running a red light, and driving "under the influence." He was alone at the time. Ron dragged himself out of bed and made it to the police station in fifteen minutes. When he arrived, he found that Steve had been locked in a cell under constant observation. The arresting officer was worried. Steve had made some remark about not being in court the day his case was to be heard. "Why not?" asked the officer. "You going on vacation?"

"No," Steve said. "You'll read about it in the paper."

Ron was worried. Maybe Steve was thinking about suicide or about hurting Chris. He didn't ask Steve what was on his mind. Instead, he collected the several powerful guns around the house and hid them.

The police had impounded Steve's Chevy, but he got it back sometime on Monday. He didn't go to school that day or the next. He said he'd start classes again on

Wednesday. Ron left for work Wednesday morning at six; Bev left the house two hours later. Steve wasn't up yet; neither was Chris. She worked odd hours at the beauty shop and wasn't starting that afternoon until two. She left for work around one-thirty and didn't see Steve.

Ron got home from work a little later than usual that afternoon—around four-thirty. He was a bit surprised to see Steve's car in the driveway, but, then, he could never keep up with Steve's schedule. He figured that Steve was in his room doing homework or getting ready to go to work. Ron went into the kitchen, got supper started, and then walked toward Steve's bedroom. In late November, it starts getting dark around five. Steve's bedroom light usually shone under the door. It was dark. Ron was puzzled. Where the heck had Steve gone? Ron had a weird feeling. Something wasn't right. He ran into Steve's room and flicked on the light. There was Steve lying on his bed with a gunshot wound in the temple. Ron's .22 caliber gun lay on the floor. The Bible Ron had bought for Steve was there on the bed, with a suicide note folded inside.

> *I am tired. Tired of everything that has happened to me from seven years ago to now. Everything that has happened has taken its toll on me and my mind. I am tired of fighting. You might ask why. But that cannot be answered by anyone, because there is no one who knows the real me. There isn't just one reason but many reasons for my downfall. But I am taking that all with me now. . . .*

When Bev pulled into the driveway an hour later, she noticed that the big light on the side of the house was on. It lit up the whole driveway and wasn't usually on unless they were having company. She wasn't expecting anyone.

The light made her uneasy. Before she had turned off the car, Ron came running out of the house, followed by a nun. Bev knew something was wrong. She braced herself.

As gently as he could, Ron told her that Steve was dead. He had put a gun to his head and pulled the trigger. Then Ron broke down. It was the first time in twenty-five years Bev had ever seen him cry. All she could think of was why *she* wasn't crying. What was wrong with *her*? Didn't she have any feelings? Dazed, she put her arm around Ron, and together they walked into the house.

All Bev wanted was to see Steve. When she reached his bedroom door, it was closed. The paramedics refused to let her in. "What do you mean, I can't go in?" she asked. "I'm a nurse. I'm used to seeing dead people." The paramedics wouldn't budge. Bev didn't push. She was too numb. She couldn't cry. She could barely talk. She never saw Steve again.

BEV AND RON found out later that Steve had taken almost all of his belongings, emptied them into garbage bags, and placed them in front of the house for Wednesday's garbage pickup. Then, sometime Wednesday morning, he had walked over to two friends' mailboxes and left an envelope in each one. Each boy found one hundred dollars and a note telling him: "Have a good time on me."

When Bev and Ron went to pick out the casket, all she could think about was what clothes Steve would wear. There's nothing, she thought. He had thrown away everything but what he had had on when he'd shot himself. When she told the funeral director her son had no clothes, he opened up a big closet filled with suits of all sizes. "Help yourself," he suggested. No way. Steve was a kid who wouldn't have his senior picture taken because he didn't want to buy a suit. He'd never wear a suit that wasn't his. Bev chose to have a closed casket. Steve would have wanted it that way.

THE FIRST YEAR after Steve's suicide was a nightmare. Bev and Ron managed to go to work, but that was about all. Bev says she wouldn't have eaten if it hadn't been for Ron's coaxing and good meals. She felt tired all the time, as if someone were pushing her down. Her back and shoulders ached constantly; her heart hurt. Either she fell asleep and then woke up a few hours later, unable to go back to sleep, or she couldn't sleep at all. She felt like a zombie most of the time.

During that first year, Bev dreamed about Steve only twice. She had the first dream seven months after he died. Men were telling her that they would find Steve, that he had just run away. Bev woke up crying Steve's name over and over again. She had the second dream two weeks before the first anniversary of Steve's suicide. In it, she walked into Steve's bedroom and noticed that something was missing. It was as if Steve had come and taken it. Bev says she knew then that Steve was really gone. This time she woke up crying Ron's name.

Ron and Bev drew closer together after Steve's suicide. Unlike many parents of suicide victims, they didn't blame each other for what had happened. They talked more than they had in years, sharing their grief and their unanswered questions: Had Steve decided to kill himself after he was arrested? Was that the last straw? Or had he decided to live it up one more time on a wild weekend because he knew it would be his last? They read and reread Steve's suicide note for clues.

Bev and Ron went through all of Steve's books and

papers. Maybe he had underlined something in his psychology book or in his Bible. Why had he done it? What had happened seven years ago? Who was the "real" Steve, and what were the reasons for his downfall? They talked to Steve's friends. The search continued.

Bev and Ron joined two groups during that first year —Compassionate Friends and LOSS. Compassionate Friends helps parents cope with the death of a child. LOSS serves survivors of suicide . . . parents, spouses, siblings, and friends. Between the two groups, the Geskes attended three meetings each month. Slowly, they began to work through their grief. They learned how to share their feelings with others. They started paying more attention to their own needs, especially at stressful times like Steve's birthday and holidays. Both Bev and Ron tried to believe that someday they would come to accept what had happened.

Neither Bev nor Ron ever thought about selling their home. It was theirs. They had raised their children there. They would stay. But Bev had a rough time going into Steve's bedroom for over a year. If the door was closed, she got spooked. What was on the other side? She begged Ron and Chris to leave it open.

Then, sometime after that first year, Bev decided to turn Steve's bedroom into her office. It would be a place where she could sit quietly and read or just think. Bev feels closest to Steve in his room. She spends a lot of her free time there. It's her room now.

Maybe three years after Steve's suicide, Bev and Ron stopped searching for clues. They stopped going to the cemetery every week. Steve had made up his mind to kill himself for his own reasons—reasons they will never understand.

But the pain still comes. Bev's voice wavers and her eyes fill with tears when she talks about Steve's having nothing of his own to wear at his own funeral. She cries every time she hears "Amazing Grace." And she still needs to stay home from work on the anniversary of Steve's death. (The anniversary of a suicide is often the most difficult time for parents and other family members. It brings back the nightmare of the suicide, forcing survivors to relive all of the emotions that overwhelmed them when they first found out.) Bev goes to an early mass, visits Steve's grave, and usually goes shopping with a friend.

Late autumn is the hardest time for Ron. That's when it starts getting dark around five. The darkness reminds him of the light that should have been on in Steve's bedroom.

PARENTS like Ron and Bev would give anything to be able to talk to their kids one more time. If only they could. Then they could ask all of those unanswered questions. They could find out why . . . why their children decided that life was more painful than death.

# (6)

# Over the Edge:
# Talks with
# Suicide Attempters

**D**o you know anyone who has attempted suicide? If you do, you're not alone. An estimated 500,000 teenagers —that's half a million—attempt suicide every year. What are these suicide attempters like? Are they looking for a dramatic way to get attention, or are they crying out for help? Do they really want to die?

Talking to teens who have attempted suicide is one good way to begin answering these questions. While they may be unsure of themselves and confused, they can help shed some light on why suicide has become an accepted "way out" for so many kids.

KATE WAS hospitalized the first time because her family therapist was sure that she was going to kill herself. The following interview was recorded toward the end of her second hospitalization. She was nineteen.

INTERVIEWER:   Tell me about your hospitalizations.

KATE:   I was in the hospital the first time from May twenty-seventh to October fifth of last year. After ten months at home, I came back again.

INTERVIEWER:   What led to your coming into the hospital the first time?

KATE:   My family and I were seeing a family therapist. The more I talked about the things that were bothering me, the more depressed I got. I decided that after I graduated from high school I was going to kill myself. I was going to graduate because my parents wanted me to. Then I was going to kill myself. I had a lot of problems. I wasn't getting along with my dad. I wanted his approval and wasn't getting it. And I broke up with my boyfriend. I couldn't handle that at all. I was totally lost without him. I was also scared about going to college. I didn't feel I was made for college. And then I started thinking about my abortion. I felt real guilty about that.

INTERVIEWER:   When did you have the abortion?

KATE:   I had it the year before I decided to kill myself. But I had totally put it out of my mind. I tried not to think about it.

INTERVIEWER:   And the breakup with your boyfriend and the therapy stirred it up again?

KATE: Um-hmm.

INTERVIEWER: Did you talk to any of your friends about your feelings?

KATE: Yes, I talked to three or four friends. They didn't believe me. They thought I was joking when I said I wanted to kill myself. To them, it looked like I was having a good time. That's because I was drinking a lot. But I was using the drinking to cover up my feelings. So my friends didn't take me seriously.

INTERVIEWER: How were you going to kill yourself?

KATE: I was going to graduate, which I did, and then that Sunday at a graduation party I was going to tell all my family good-bye. And then that Monday I was going to kill myself by carbon-monoxide poisoning in the garage with the car. That's how I was going to do it.

INTERVIEWER: Did you ever know anybody who had killed herself that way?

KATE: No. I think I read it in the newspaper.

INTERVIEWER: If you hadn't come to the hospital, do you think you would have done it?

KATE: Yes, because I had tried before. I had taken pills, like speed, and then drank a lot. I was real sick many times.

INTERVIEWER: Did you talk to anybody at school? A teacher? A guidance counselor?

KATE: I talked to one of my teachers and to my counselor. She was the one who recommended this counseling place for my whole family.

INTERVIEWER: Do you think she knew you were going to kill yourself?

KATE: I don't think so. I think she thought I was really sad and depressed, that I needed time away from people.

INTERVIEWER: And you never told her that you wanted to die?

KATE: No. I did tell some of my friends but not the counselor or the teacher.

INTERVIEWER: What did you accomplish during your first stay in the hospital?

KATE: The first month I was happy and everything, trying to make everybody think I was fine. And then I got real depressed. I started talking about a lot of my secrets that I had kept inside.

INTERVIEWER: Like the abortion?

KATE: Like being molested when I was seven and raped twice when I was in eighth grade. And that I was still angry at my father.

INTERVIEWER: Your father wasn't the one who molested you, was he?

KATE: No, it was a friend's father.

INTERVIEWER: And the rapes? Were those people you knew?

KATE: Yeah, I knew them in grade school. I was so scared of them after it happened that I went to a different high school. I was terrified.

INTERVIEWER: Did your family know about these things?

KATE: No, not until I got into the hospital. I finally told my parents everything.

INTERVIEWER: What was their reaction?

KATE: They felt real badly for me. At first, they didn't know how to feel or what to say. My dad was real angry, especially about my abortion. And they were real upset that I didn't feel I could go to them and talk to them. But I felt they had certain values, beliefs. I didn't feel they would like me if I went and told them this stuff. They would really hate my guts and wouldn't want me as a daughter.

INTERVIEWER: And you started to feel like killing yourself again after letting all this out?

KATE: Yeah. I just didn't want to feel any more pain.

INTERVIEWER: Where would you be if you weren't in the hospital right now?

KATE: In my grave.

INTERVIEWER: You would be dead?

KATE: Yeah.

INTERVIEWER: You would have succeeded in killing yourself?

KATE: Right.

INTERVIEWER: Other teenagers who read this might think you're just a regular kid who doesn't really sound that depressed. How do you do that? How do you appear so together when you're actually so desperate inside?

KATE: It's my cover. I always smile and look real happy when I'm depressed. I make everybody think that I'm just fine. That way, they'll leave me alone.

INTERVIEWER: But people here aren't leaving you alone. Does it help that they're taking you so seriously?

KATE: At first, I wished they didn't take me so seriously. I was obsessed with killing myself. But after a few weeks, I was told that I had to start working on my anger and letting negative feelings out. I started feeling less tense or something. I don't know exactly what.

INTERVIEWER: You let it out.

KATE: Yeah, I started to do that. But I have a whole lot more to do.

INTERVIEWER: So, before you would cover up the anger with a smile?

KATE: I still do that sometimes. But now I can tell when I'm doing it and try to change it.

INTERVIEWER: Are you learning how to turn things around so that you're not feeling so depressed?

KATE: No, I haven't learned how to do that yet, but I've learned how to tell people that I'm feeling a certain way.

INTERVIEWER: What happened after you left the hospital the first time?

KATE: I went home, and things were going fine for the first three months. Then I started drinking more and taking speed. I felt I was too fat. I still think that. Then it seemed like I was seeing less and less of my friends. I'd call them up, and they didn't have much desire to talk to me or to go out. They knew I'd been in a psychiatric hospital, and that scared them away. It was real hard for me because some of the friends I thought were really close to me and cared about me (even when I was in here) deserted me when I got home. I couldn't take that.

INTERVIEWER: What were they afraid of?

KATE: I think they were scared of the fact that I was in a psychiatric hospital with crazy people. They didn't know how I was going to act and didn't want the burden of me going nuts on them or killing myself while I was with them. It was really hard. In a lot of ways, I felt I knew more than they did. I felt more grown up. I found out a lot more about myself and other people at the same time.

INTERVIEWER: So you started to feel lonely, not having your old friends. Was that the primary thing that was getting you depressed?

KATE: That was the start of it.

INTERVIEWER: You were in counseling as an outpatient, weren't you?

KATE: Yeah.

INTERVIEWER: And were you able to talk about these feeling in counseling?

KATE: Some of them. But I wanted everyone to think that I was doing well. When I left the hospital, I was this great patient, someone that people would remember as real positive. I didn't want anyone to see that inside I was starting to fall apart again.

INTERVIEWER:   What else was going on that got you more and more depressed at home?

KATE:   I had just started college and was having a hard time. I didn't know how to make new friends. All my old friends had just left me, and I was supposed to make new ones. I started a job at a nursery school and had a real hard time working with little kids because of my abortion. And then my father and I started getting along worse and worse. We started arguing and got to the point where we didn't even speak anymore.

INTERVIEWER:   Did you try to kill yourself when you were home between hospitalizations?

KATE:   I got to the point where I wasn't feeling anything. It was like I pushed all the pain away. I just didn't want to deal with it anymore. Then I started thinking about killing myself. But I wasn't feeling anything so I tried to feel pain. I burned myself with an iron a couple of times.

INTERVIEWER:   Were you alone when you did that?

KATE:   Yes, I was alone. I knew what I was doing but I did it, anyway. And then I did real risky things, like use the hair dryer with the water running. If I got electrocuted, I got electrocuted. And I started driving like a maniac when I was alone in the car.

INTERVIEWER:   If you had died, people would have thought it was accidental.

KATE:   That way, my parents wouldn't have felt so guilty.

INTERVIEWER:   How do you think they would feel if you died?

KATE: Pretty sad, I guess. I don't know. If I did it intentionally, they would feel they didn't do enough for me or they weren't around when I needed them. But it's not that way. That's why I thought about writing a letter and telling them it wasn't their fault. It was just me. I couldn't find something that kept me happy, something I wanted to live for. I had given myself eight weeks to see if I could be happier. If I couldn't do that, I told the counselor that I was going to quit seeing him. Then I started talking about doing things like the hair dryer stuff. I mentioned writing a will and a letter explaining why I wanted to die.

INTERVIEWER: How did you feel when your counselor said you had to go back into the hospital?

KATE: I was shocked. And I couldn't change his mind. He said I could sign myself in or he would do something to put me into the hospital. I signed myself in.

INTERVIEWER: What have you done in the hospital this time?

KATE: I learned how to be assertive. I'm working on my anger and trying to find new ways of dealing with my problems.

INTERVIEWER: How do you feel right now about hurting or killing yourself?

KATE: I think about it, usually when something is real hard for me to handle. I get impulsive and feel like strangling myself or something like that. Last night, I was drawing pictures and I drew a picture of a hanging man and a broken heart. I wasn't doing it consciously. I was just drawing. I guess somewhere— I *know* somewhere—that I still feel like that at times.

But that's a side I have to deal with. Maybe once or twice a week I feel really good. But it's rare, and it seems like those times only last for a little bit. The bad times last so much longer.

INTERVIEWER: What do you think your chances of surviving are?

KATE: I think they're better now than a month ago.

INTERVIEWER: What do you think of death?

KATE: I drew a picture of death once. I picture it as peaceful and happy and content.

INTERVIEWER: You don't see it as painful?

KATE: I think life is painful.

INTERVIEWER: What do you think your funeral would be like?

KATE: I don't picture many people coming . . . just my parents, grandparents, a few other relatives, and some friends I grew up with. But I do picture the dress I'll wear. And I know that I want one yellow rose with me. That's my favorite flower.

INTERVIEWER: It's almost like someone visualizes a wedding.

KATE: I always get yellow roses on good occasions. My funeral would be a good occasion.

INTERVIEWER: Are you worried that you have to be in a hospital all the time in order not to hurt yourself?

KATE: It scares me. I wonder whether I'm always going to be like this or whether there's going to be a time when I'll finally be able to be independent and on my own . . . to have good times and enjoy them.

INTERVIEWER: Does talking help? Does talking about your feelings help?

KATE: It hurts a lot, but it helps.

———

NATALIE WAS fourteen when she attempted suicide. She has been hospitalized twice. Her father admitted her the first time; a year later, she checked herself in. This interview was recorded toward the end of her second hospitalization.

INTERVIEWER: What was it like growing up in your house?

NATALIE: I have a sister and I don't like her. She's nineteen now. She moved out of the house five months ago. I really dislike her. That's a big part of why I'm in this hospital. I refuse to get along with her. She's close with Papa, and I guess that hurts.

INTERVIEWER: Have you always had problems with her?

NATALIE: For about five years . . . since she started getting interested in boys. My parents would go out on bowling nights, and she would have parties. If I called my parents and told them what was going on, she'd beat me. She grabbed my hair and scratched the back of my neck with her long nails. I still have scars.

INTERVIEWER: Your sister is out of the house now?

NATALIE: Yeah, but she comes home every weekend to get money from my father. It seems as if he likes her more than me. He always bails her out. She has her own apartment. He pays for part of the rent, the insurance, and for all of her good clothes.

INTERVIEWER:  And that makes you angry?

NATALIE:  Yeah, because I don't get it. I don't get half of what she does.

INTERVIEWER:  Material things?

NATALIE:  Material things and love. He's always liked her better.

INTERVIEWER:  Have you ever talked to your dad about your feelings?

NATALIE:  I said that he liked her more, and he denied it.

INTERVIEWER:  Where does your mom fit in?

NATALIE:  My mom's a manic-depressive. She just falls between the cracks.

INTERVIEWER:  Is she on medication?

NATALIE:  Yeah, she's on lithium. And she's been like this ever since I can remember. People tell me that's why I'm unhappy. The first time I was hospitalized, I was really angry with her. But not anymore. I don't think my mother is the problem at all.

INTERVIEWER:  What's it like when she stops taking her medication?

NATALIE:  It's hard for the whole family. She does stupid and crazy things. She got angry once when my father was working a lot, so she went and cut up all of his money. Then she parked the car under a broken garage door. The door slammed into the car.

INTERVIEWER:  How many times has she been hospitalized?

NATALIE: Countless. I can remember missing at least two or three Christmases because she was either in the hospital or very sick. When she gets sick, she hates the family and tells us that we're not up to her level. I almost hit her a couple of times. But I didn't. My father would beat me. Besides, I knew she wasn't in her right mind.

INTERVIEWER: It must be hard for all of you . . . your dad, too.

NATALIE: My father knew what he was getting into when he married her. She had already been in the hospital at least twice. He's a rock, anyway.

INTERVIEWER: He doesn't show his emotions?

NATALIE: He gets annoyed but he doesn't break down and cry. It just doesn't seem to bother him that much.

INTERVIEWER: When were you in the hospital the first time?

NATALIE: Around this time last year.

INTERVIEWER: Did you try to commit suicide?

NATALIE: Yeah, I tried twice. I took my grandmother's pills, something for depression.

INTERVIEWER: How many pills did you take?

NATALIE: Around twenty the first time. My father found me in the morning. I couldn't stand up. He took me to the hospital to have my stomach pumped. Then he took me to my aunt's house. That was on a Monday. I slept the rest of the day and all day Tuesday.

INTERVIEWER:  Why did he take you to your aunt's house?

NATALIE:  Because he had to work, and my mom was in the hospital. I tried to kill myself again on Wednesday. I took the rest of my grandmother's pills. Then I drank milk of magnesia, Liquid Plumber, and peroxide. I passed out. My father and aunt brought me here to this hospital.

INTERVIEWER:  Why did you try to kill yourself?

NATALIE:  My boyfriend had broken up with me. And my best friend was away. I had no way of reaching her.

INTERVIEWER:  How did she react when she found out about your suicide attempt?

NATALIE:  She was real mad at me. She doesn't know how to show emotions, but she almost hit me. I'm not saying she doesn't listen to me. But she takes my unhappiness personally. She thinks I don't believe that she cares about me. I don't mean to make her feel that way. None of this is her fault.

INTERVIEWER:  Did you tell anybody you were thinking of killing yourself?

NATALIE:  No. I always thought about suicide. But I was never serious about it until then. My parents believed I was serious, too. But my sister said I was just trying to get attention. The more I talk about her, the more upset I get. It makes me want to leave this room.

INTERVIEWER:  Did you think about what death would be like?

NATALIE:  I know that I'd go to hell.

INTERVIEWER:   Are you religious?

NATALIE:   No, but I believe in heaven and hell. I'm not sure people are going to cry when I die. I don't think my life is worth as much as the next guy. I do nothing with my life. I go to school . . . fool around. I'm a good listener, but that doesn't mean I know the right answers. Most of the time I don't.

INTERVIEWER:   Did you want to be saved?

NATALIE:   No, I thought I had it planned. Both times. But I made a mistake. I left a pill somewhere the first time, and my father found it. The second time, I threw everything up. My father tried to get me something to eat on the way to the hospital. I couldn't eat but I still wanted to kill myself. I went into the washroom and tried to slash my wrists on the metal edge of the sink. That didn't work, either. What's strange is that I hate the sight of blood. It makes me totally sick. I must have been out of it because I'd never try to kill myself that way.

INTERVIEWER:   Do you like school?

NATALIE:   I like going to school to see kids. I get along with them. My problems are with adults. And I feel really ignorant in the classroom.

INTERVIEWER:   Are there any subjects that you like?

NATALIE:   I like reading. I like scary books by Stephen King.

INTERVIEWER:   What kind of grades did you get when you were younger?

NATALIE:  Not bad. But I do remember getting yelled at often because I goofed around and didn't know how to spell my name. That was the only problem I can remember until fifth grade. Then I sluffed off. Work started getting harder and harder. I don't have the attention span for it.

INTERVIEWER:  What was your father's reaction?

NATALIE:  He was mad and got very, very strict with me. I had to be in earlier than all the other kids. I rebelled against my father a lot.

INTERVIEWER:  Did you have a grammar school yearbook?

NATALIE:  No.

INTERVIEWER:  If you had, what would have been written under your picture?

NATALIE:  "The most blunt."

INTERVIEWER:  You mean, saying what you really feel?

NATALIE:  Right. I don't like to "B.S." If I don't like someone, I'm not going to play kissy face with them. I don't like to play games.

INTERVIEWER:  What else would have been written about you in the yearbook?

NATALIE:  That I know how to take care of myself on the street.

INTERVIEWER:  Where did you learn how to be street-wise?

NATALIE:  From my girl friend and my father. My father is the same way I am. He doesn't take anything from anyone. He's a real fighter. So is my girl friend.

INTERVIEWER:   Is she the one who was away the day you decided to kill yourself?

NATALIE:   Yeah.

INTERVIEWER:   Have you been friends for a long time?

NATALIE:   For four years. When we first met, I was a wall-flower. I stayed in the house all the time. I was scared of everybody and everything. I had gotten in a fight with a girl, and she beat me. I was embarrassed. And I stayed in the house for a year. Then I met Karen. She didn't like my style at all. She taught me how to fight.

INTERVIEWER:   Is that something you need to know how to do?

NATALIE:   I feel I do. I'm in a gang.

INTERVIEWER:   A street gang?

NATALIE:   Yeah.

INTERVIEWER:   Why do you belong?

NATALIE:   I don't consider it a real gang. We don't go around shooting people. We just defend our neighborhood. All my good friends are in it. We're known as real troublesome kids. My parents tell me I've changed. They said I used to be nice and lovable but that now I'm cold, too independent, and too mouthy to adults. They're right about the adults. I have a real problem with them. But I get along fine with my friends. I feel I'm a decent person as far as my personality goes. But I don't like myself at all in other areas.

INTERVIEWER: What don't you like about yourself?

NATALIE: I'm fat. I think I'm ugly. And I don't have my own mind with guys. They hurt me and make me feel like I have nothing left to live for.

INTERVIEWER: That's what set things off a year ago?

NATALIE: Yeah.

INTERVIEWER: Why were you hospitalized this second time? Did you attempt suicide again?

NATALIE: No. I was going to, but I wasn't alone enough. I was on the run, living with my friends. I didn't feel right having one of my friends find me dead. What would they do? Besides, my father would probably kill them.

INTERVIEWER: Did you run away from home?

NATALIE: Yeah. I ran away because I was unhappy. The day before I left, my father beat me. I lost ten dollars and was about ten minutes late coming home. My father dragged me off the bed and punched me in the face. Then he hit me with something and kicked me once. I was bleeding all over the place.

INTERVIEWER: All because you lost the money and were late?

NATALIE: A couple of days before, I was five minutes late, then I was late again. It all built up. My father decided I needed a beating. I think he thought that would put me in my place.

INTERVIEWER: But it had the opposite effect.

NATALIE: Right. I ran away.

INTERVIEWER: How did you get back in the hospital?

NATALIE:    I checked myself in. I'd been on the run for eight days. I was thinking of killing myself but didn't want to lay that on my friends. I decided I needed help.

INTERVIEWER:    How are you feeling now?

NATALIE:    I still feel like killing myself sometimes. But I don't know how to say that to people here in the hospital without losing their trust in me.

INTERVIEWER:    But soon you're going to be out of here and on your own. What's going to happen the next time you have a fight with your father or a problem with a boyfriend?

NATALIE:    I'm not sure. I don't like lying and saying I'll work it out on my own. I don't know if I'm ever going to try to kill myself again. I really don't know.

---

### CONCLUSION

Neither Natalie nor Kate is certain about the future. Both girls still feel suicidal from time to time; they both have problems left to work out.

What is encouraging is that Natalie and Kate have gone for help. Both girls realized that they were in trouble and needed the structure, supervision, and counseling that a hospital can provide. Natalie and Kate have established connections to professionals who care about them and who have their best interests in mind.

There is no way of knowing for certain whether Natalie and Kate will live or die. But the odds on living are now in their favor.

Depressed/suicidal teens who get effective help have

a better than 80 percent chance for a full recovery. Chances are good that Natalie and Kate will decide that living is less painful than dying, that life offers more for them than death.

# ( 7 )

# *When You're the First to Know: Helping a Friend through a Problem*

**I**T'S SCARY when someone you know is depressed, maybe even suicidal. Talking about your own "bad" feelings is hard enough. Talking about someone else's problems may seem impossible. How can you know the "right" things to say or do when a friend has a serious problem? What if you mess up? You could cause your friend to do something horrible. You'd walk around feeling guilty for a long time. So why take a chance? Why get involved? Besides, how do you know if your friend is really depressed? Maybe s/he is joking around. Or maybe s/he is just trying to get your attention. How can you find out what's really going on? What can you do once you know?

JOSH STARTED giving things away—his books, his calculators, his good pens. He wouldn't be needing them anymore. Josh had had enough. He couldn't stand the pressure. All the pushing to stay at the top of his class, to get all *A*'s, to get into the best college. He was tired. The pain was too much. Josh had decided to kill himself.

He walked home from school alone, working out the details of his suicide. He would rig up a noose in the basement and hang himself when no one was home.

"Hey, Josh," his friend, Dylan, yelled, interrupting his thoughts.

*Why did Dylan have to bother him now?* Josh kept walking.

"Wait up!" Dylan said again, as he ran to catch up with Josh.

Josh didn't stop.

"What's wrong with you?" Dylan asked, out of breath, once he'd caught up.

"Nothing."

"Why didn't you wait?"

"Didn't feel like it."

"Didn't feel like it? Well, screw you!"

"Yeah, screw me. That's what I'm about to do."

Dylan was surprised. Why was Josh acting so hostile? "Something bothering you?" he asked.

"Yeah . . . lots of things."

"Like what?"

"Like I've had it up to here," he said, pointing to his neck.

"What could possibly be wrong with you?" Dylan asked. "Your life is all set."

"That's what you think," Josh mumbled.

"That's what I know. You've got it all together. Valedictorian of the senior class . . . Harvard freshman. What more could you ask for?"

"Plenty."

"Come on, Josh, you're acting crazy."

"I feel crazy. I'm all messed up inside." He paused. Should he even bother?

"You? Messed up? Come on, you've got to be joking."

Fine. He'd tell him. "I'm going to kill myself."

Dylan looked at his friend. He couldn't be serious. Not Josh.

"I mean it. I want to die," Josh said, as if reading Dylan's thoughts.

"That's the dumbest thing I've ever heard."

"Dumb to you, maybe . . . ."

Dylan started to laugh. "Here's Mr. Together telling me he wants to die. Give me a break."

Josh was angry. "I'll give you a break," he said as he walked away. "You'll never have to deal with me again!"

Dylan stood and watched his best friend practically trip over his own feet in his hurry to get away. Josh was upset. He'd cool off. Everything would be fine.

EVERYTHING WOULD NOT be fine. Josh had taken a big risk by letting Dylan in on his problems and plan to kill himself. But Dylan hadn't taken him seriously. Dylan couldn't believe that someone who apparently had everything going for him would want to kill himself. He was sure Josh was joking. And when Josh told Dylan he was dead serious, Dylan cut him down. He told him it was the dumbest thing he'd ever heard. Dylan's inability to listen to Josh without criticizing—without judging—made Josh angry. Here he had opened up and tried to talk about his suicidal feelings, and all he'd gotten was a supposed friend who thought it was all one big joke.

What could Dylan have done differently? How could he have helped Josh?

WHEN DYLAN saw Josh giving things away, he thought it was a bit strange. What was Josh doing? Didn't he need his books, calculators, and pens?

Dylan pulled Josh aside after lunch. "Why are you giving all your stuff away?" he asked.

"Don't need it," Josh mumbled. "Don't need anything."

Dylan was confused. Josh wasn't making sense. "I don't get it," he said.

"Nobody gets it. That's the point."

Josh was talking in circles. "You sound unhappy," Dylan said.

"I'm not feeling too great. That's for sure."

"Interested in talking? If you are, I'm willing to listen."

Should he tell him? "I've had it up to here," Josh said, pointing to his neck. "The pressure is too much. My parents, school . . . myself."

Dylan felt sorry for him. "It must be rough trying to get all *A*'s."

Josh nodded.

"When I was up for Most Valuable Player of the baseball team, I was so nervous. I couldn't concentrate on hitting the ball."

"I know what you mean," Josh said sadly.

Dylan was afraid. "You're not thinking of doing anything crazy, are you?"

Josh stared down at his shoes.

"Come on, Josh, fill me in."

Okay. He'd tell him. "I'm going to kill myself."

"You're really down, aren't you?"

"Yeah." He started to cry. "I can't take it anymore."

Dylan bit the inside of his lip. He couldn't panic. Not now. He'd have to take charge. "I'm worried about you," he said sincerely.

"Thanks."

"I want to help."

"Nobody can help."

Dylan had to think fast. "How about talking to Ms. Dreiser?"

"She wouldn't understand."

"Why not try her? You might be surprised."

Josh was tired. "I can handle it. Really, I can."

"I won't leave you alone," Dylan said. "You're my best friend. I won't let you hurt yourself."

Josh was relieved. He slumped down on the floor in front of his locker, knowing that Dylan meant what he had said.

MAYBE YOU just can't get involved in helping a friend with a problem. You've tried, but emotional conflicts make you uneasy. What should you do, then, when a friend comes to you for help? Be honest. Tell your friend that you care a lot but that you aren't the right person to talk to. If you can, suggest someone else—another friend, a teacher, counselor, or parent. And, later, check up on your friend to see how things are going.

On the other hand, you may be a listener who feels comfortable helping a friend with a problem. You know you can't solve friends' problems for them but you can encourage them to open up and talk. You can find out how serious the problems are. You can show you care. And maybe you can help your friends see alternatives—different ways of making things better.

### YOUR FRIENDS ARE THE FIRST TO KNOW

When you have a problem, to whom do you talk? Your parents? A teacher? A good friend? Most teenagers turn to a good friend. Friends know where you're coming from. They know what it's like to be a teen.

Parents and teachers have a harder time remembering what it's like. They think back on their teenage years as the "best time of their lives." They've forgotten the pain of breaking up with a boyfriend or girl friend. They can't remember how much pressure there was to get good grades. They don't recall those days when being like everyone else—even if it meant doing things that felt wrong—was more important than anything. Most adults have blocked out the pain; they only remember the good times. But your friends are right there with you, trying to make some sense out of it all.

Some friends seem to know exactly what to say when you're feeling down. They listen to you and really hear what you're saying. They manage to help you see what is wrong and what to do next.

### WHAT MAKES A GOOD LISTENER?

Good listeners try to hear what you have to say. They don't order you to get rid of "bad" feelings; they accept them. They don't tell you what to do. They don't put you down or make you feel guilty. And they don't make you feel that *you* are the problem.

BECOMING A BETTER LISTENER: SHOW YOU'RE LISTENING

You can say a lot to a friend without uttering a word. How? The way you look at a friend, your posture, the way you move all give clear messages about how you're feeling.

You're not convinced? Picture this: You finally get up the nerve to tell your best friend that you think you need psychiatric help. Your whole world is caving in. Nothing is going right.

"I've got to talk to you," you say.

Your friend looks away.

"Come on, it's really important."

Your friend shuffles back and forth, flipping the pages of the book he's holding.

"I need to talk to you, and you could care less."

"Who said I don't care? Did I say that?"

"No, you didn't *say* it . . . well, not exactly. But that's what you're telling me."

What went wrong? Why did you lose faith in your friend and his interest in what you had to say? Your friend didn't make eye contact with you; he looked away. He moved around while you were talking and fidgeted with his book. His actions told you he wasn't really interested in what you were saying, even though he denied not caring.

Now imagine the same scene played differently:

"I've got to talk to you."

Your friend looks you straight in the eye.

"I think I need psychiatric help."

Your friend leans forward.

"Nothing is going right. Nothing."

Several people walk by the two of you in the school corridor. Your friend doesn't seem to notice.

"The minute I wake up, I feel sick to my stomach. The feeling never goes away."

Right off the bat, your friend showed you he was interested in what you had to say. He made eye contact but didn't stare. That made you want to keep talking. "I think I need psychiatric help." There. You said it. Would he laugh in your face? No. Instead, he leaned forward. You kept talking. Other people walked by the two of you in the school corridor, but your friend still concentrated on you and what you were saying. His actions told you that he wanted to hear more and really cared.

Nonverbal actions—facial and eye expressions, gestures, and posture—say a lot. They can tell a friend that you care and that you're listening or they can tell a friend that you don't give a darn, even if you think you do.

### MIRRORING A FRIEND'S FEELINGS[1]

You would think that friends with problems would be able to tell you exactly how they feel . . . nervous, sad, hurt, embarrassed. But when most people express their feelings, they usually don't use feeling words. They're upset and can't think clearly. And they've been trained not to talk about negative or "bad" feelings. It's no wonder that talking about problems is rough. Who wants to admit their life isn't perfect? Who wants to admit they have problems they can't solve?

[1]Dinkmeyer, Don and McKay, Gary. *The Parent's Guide: Step/Teen Systematic Training for Effective Parenting of Teens.* Circle Pines, MN: American Guidance Service, 1983.

The trick of good listening is getting people to talk about themselves and their feelings. One of the best ways to help friends understand their feelings better is to be a mirror, to reflect back the feelings you think you hear and see.

Here's how mirroring works: A good friend of yours wanted the nomination for class president but didn't get it. Looking defeated, he says: "I didn't get the nomination. There were too many people more qualified than me."

After giving yourself enough time to think about what your friend was feeling and what made him feel that way, you might say: "You're feeling *that the other kids are better than you* because you weren't nominated."

You reflected, or mirrored, your friend's hurt feelings ("You're feeling the other kids are better than you") and you told him why you thought he was feeling hurt ("because you weren't nominated"). You restated your friend's message. You reflected what he felt, and why. Feedback is what's going on here. Not repetition. If you simply repeated what was said, you'd get your friend angry in a hurry. He'd think you were nothing more than a tape recorder.

Fine, you think. You know *what* a friend is feeling, and *why*. But what do you say? How do you mirror? Some people like using a pattern: You feel ——— because ———. But don't think you're locked into this pattern. You can change "You feel" to "You're feeling," "You sound," "You seem," or anything else that works. You can change "because" to "about," "with," "at," or "by." The important thing is that you catch the meaning behind the words and restate what you think you hear. And you'll want to mirror what you *think* your friend is *feeling*, and *why*. Unless you have psychic powers, you can't read your friend's mind. So don't *tell* him what's going on. Mirror what you *think* has been said. If you're checking out a hunch—not playing a know-it-all—you'll have a much better chance of getting your friend to talk.

Here is an example of how mirroring works.

JANE: I don't see why my mother won't let me go to the party.

SUE: You're angry because your mom won't let you go.

JANE: I sure am! She's so unfair.

SUE: You think she's not treating you right.

JANE: I know she's not. She said I had to finish my homework, and I did. She doesn't believe me.

SUE: You're upset because she doesn't think you're telling the truth.

JANE: She never believes me.

SUE: Can you show her your assignment notebook and the completed homework?

JANE: Maybe.

SUE: You're not sure whether she'll change her mind.

JANE: My mother is very stubborn.

SUE: That frustrates you, because it's hard to get her to see things your way.

JANE: You said it! But maybe if I cool down and talk to her nicely, she'll let me go to the party.

Mirroring takes practice. But the more you practice, the better you'll be. If you want to help your friends share their feelings, try mirroring. It works with parents, teachers, brothers, and sisters, too.

### WHEN A FRIEND WON'T TALK

Even the best listeners run into people who won't talk. What next? First, you might try making a guess about *nonverbal* messages . . . eye and facial expressions, gestures, and posture. If your friend is smiling, or gritting her teeth, or fidgeting, say something like: "You seem happy." "Looks like you're angry." "You seem really nervous." Your friend may tell you you're off base. Or your "guess" may open up a good conversation. "I'm nervous. You can say that again! My parents are going to kill me when they see these grades."

Another way to get a conversation going is to ask a question. "How's it going with you and Marc?" You may get a one word answer: "Okay," "Great," "Fine"—all ways of saying "I don't feel like talking." Or your simple question could start an interesting talk.

"How's it going with Marc?"

"Not so hot. He's never interested in doing anything."

"You're bored because of it?"

"I'm losing interest—fast!"

"Sounds like you're thinking of breaking up with him."

"Yeah, but if I do that, who is there left to go out with?"

Once the listener asked a direct question and got an answer, she used mirroring to reflect what she thought her friend was feeling and why. Mirroring encouraged her friend to talk more about her boyfriend and why she was

unhappy with him. It showed her friend that she was
listening carefully and that she cared.

### HOW TO ASK GOOD QUESTIONS

You've keyed in on a friend's nonverbal messages—
her dejected look and lack of energy—and "guessed" that
she is depressed. Almost inaudibly, she admits you're
right and mumbles something about "hurting so much
she wishes she could die." You give yourself enough time
to word your response and then say, "You must be very
unhappy if you're talking about death." Your friend
doesn't answer. She probably knows that you're willing
to listen, but doesn't have the strength to talk. You can
wait her out or you can try asking some good questions.
Asking questions is the key to finding out more information and to exploring possible alternatives for solving the
problem.

Questions that can be answered with a "yes," "no,"
or defensive response won't get you anywhere.

"Are you still having trouble at home?"

"Yes."

"Why don't you talk to your parents?"

"I can't."

"Do you think you should talk to a counselor?"

"No."

Questions like these don't encourage a friend to
share information. They may even cut off your attempt at
conversation.

Questions that *do* encourage sharing often begin with
*where, when, what, who, which,* or *how.*

"*What* is making you feel so down?"

"*When* did your parents separate?"

*"How* are you going to talk to them?"

These kinds of questions usually keep a conversation going. They ask for information that you need or for feelings that your friend can share. Yet asking a good question does not guarantee that your friend will open up. The *way* you ask the question—your tone of voice and the nonverbal messages you send—are very important. No one who is challenged is likely to want to talk. But even so, the tone of your voice and your nonverbal messages can fail, even if your question is a good one and your heart is in the right place.

EXPLORING WAYS OF SOLVING A FRIEND'S PROBLEM

You've paid attention to nonverbal messages, mirrored a friend's feelings, and asked some good questions. Both you and your friend know and understand what is wrong. Now it's time to explore different ways of solving the problem or for you to suggest that your friend talk to someone else. You're not superhuman. Sometimes other peoples' problems are just too big to handle. If that's the case, don't leave your friend up in the air. Tell him you're glad he's confided in you and hope that he trusts you. Then be honest and tell him you think he should talk to someone else. Help him consider different people and choose the "right" one. And set a time when the two of you can get back together to talk.

If you feel comfortable working with your friend and helping him look at possible solutions to his problem, ask him something like, "Do you want to look at some possible ways of solving the problem?" If he says "yes," you and he can make some headway. (If he's not so enthusiastic, tell him you understand and offer your help for another time.) What next? How about brainstorming? That's right. Ask your friend to think of all the possible ways he could solve his problem.

"I could kill myself."

"I could talk to a counselor."

"I could do nothing."

"I could beg my parents to get back together."

That's great, you're thinking. But what if your friend can't come up with any ideas? Try asking if someone else he knows has the same problem. "What if Paul felt the same way? What would you tell him?" Or try reversing roles. Have your friend take the role of the person he's having a problem with. You take his role. This gives you the chance to show how you would handle the problem. Or make a suggestion. Now, that's different from giving advice. Advice tells someone what he should do. A suggestion offers an idea that can be accepted or rejected. "What do you think would happen if you talked to a counselor?" "Have you thought about joining a group with other kids?" Once there are a variety of possible solutions up for discussion, ask your friend to evaluate each one.

"What do you think about seeing a counselor?"

"Well, the idea makes me nervous, but it might be worth a try."

"What about killing yourself? Do you have a plan?"

"No. Every time I think about pills or sitting in a closed garage with the car running, I get sick to my stomach."

"Doesn't sound like you want to kill yourself, because the methods make you sick."

*(Mirroring)*

"I guess you're right."

"You talked about begging your parents not to get a divorce."

"Yeah, but that won't work. They're not going to change their minds because of me or anyone else."

"Well, you said something about doing nothing. How's that sound?"

"Not so hot. I can't stand feeling like this. I want to scream."

"It sounds like you want to do something to make yourself feel better."

*(Mirroring)*

"I guess seeing someone is the best idea."

"You don't seem very convinced."

*(Mirroring)*

"I'm nervous. I told you that before. What if he thinks I'm really messed up and wants to put me in one of those hospitals?"

"You're afraid he'll want to put you away."

*(Mirroring)*

"Yeah, it scares me. I know I'm messed up, but I'm not some weirdo."

"How could the counselor help you?"

"I don't know. He probably can't."

"You don't think there's any way out of the pain."

*(Mirroring)*

"That's the way it feels."

"What would you like the counselor to do?"

"I'd like him to help me feel happy again. I used to feel so happy. . . ."

"Are you willing to find out which counselor to see?"

"I'll try."

"It doesn't sound as if you're that serious about trying."

*(Mirroring)*

"I am . . . I'll try."

"Why don't I call you tomorrow and see how you feel?"

Once someone chooses a possible alternative to his problem, it's a great idea to ask good questions and help clarify the reasons for the choice. Where in this conversation did the listener ask her friend to clarify the choice? If you said when she asked, "How could the counselor help you?" you were right. Notice that that question and the one following it begin with *How* and *What*—two words that usually begin open questions, questions that encourage an answer. Did you also notice that the listener asked her friend to follow up on her choice ("Are you willing to find out which counselor to see?") and that she set a time to talk again? That way, she let her friend know that there would be a chance to see how the choice was working.

### SUMMING UP

When most people think of communication, they think of talking. But listening is really the most important part of communication between two people. If you want to help friends sort through their feelings and focus on what needs to be done, there are some good listening techniques to follow:

### PAYING ATTENTION TO NONVERBAL MESSAGES

You and your friends say a lot without ever uttering a word. Facial and eye expressions, posture, and gestures all give clear messages about how you or a friend is feeling. As a good listener, you'll want to pay attention to the nonverbal signals you send. If a friend feels that you're interested in what is being said by the way you look and act, chances are better that you will have a good conversation.

Keying in on the nonverbal messages a friend is giving you is also important. Sometimes, particularly when a friend isn't talking, you can make a "guess" about feelings, based on nonverbal actions. Your friend may tell you that your "guess" is way off base, or your "guess" may open up the conversation. Paying attention to nonverbal messages is one good listening skill.

### MIRRORING

As we've discussed, one of the best ways to help a hurting friend "see" what s/he really is feeling is to mirror, or reflect, what you think you hear and see. When you mirror, you restate a friend's message without adding any of your own feelings to it. Mirroring is a way of checking out feelings, not a way for you to play a know-it-all.

A lot of people like using a pattern when they mirror. But the pattern is just a device that can easily be changed. The important thing is to catch the meaning behind what a friend is saying and to restate what you think you hear.

### ASKING GOOD QUESTIONS

Asking good questions is the key to finding out more information from a friend and to exploring possible solutions. Good questions encourage a friend to share and often begin with *Where, When, What, Who, Which,* or *How.* These kinds of questions usually keep a conversation going. However, they don't guarantee that a friend will talk. The *way* you ask the question—your tone of voice and the nonverbal messages you send—is very important.

It can make the difference between opening and blocking a friend's eagerness to share information with you.

Good questions also help a friend explore ways of solving a problem. They can ask a friend to brainstorm or to reverse roles. Good questions can also allow you to make a suggestion. ("Have you thought about . . . ?")

Finally, good questions help a friend clarify the reasons why a particular plan of action was chosen. Sometimes a friend might even decide on a different plan after looking carefully at the first choice.

IF A FRIEND IS TALKING ABOUT SUICIDE
1. Listen without preaching; don't lecture—mirror what you think you hear and see.
2. Ask good questions ("How do you plan on killing yourself?" "What do you think it would be like to be dead?")
3. Let the friend know she/he is not alone ("I have felt some of these things, too.")
4. Take charge; don't leave a suicidal friend alone.
5. Get help; call a teacher, counselor, or parent, or the police or suicide hot line.

# (8)

# *It's Good to Know You've Got a Friend*

**A**RE YOU LUCKY enough to have a good friend who is there for you whenever you have a problem? Teens who think seriously about suicide usually don't. They feel all alone, with no one to talk to. Friendship can make the difference between teenagers who attempt suicide and those who do not. A good friend can often help a troubled teen make it through the pain, though there are never any guarantees.

After a friend of his killed herself, Rick started thinking about suicide all the time. He almost put a gun to his head on a hunting trip with his father not long after his friend's funeral. He didn't go through with it, but he didn't feel any less depressed. He would wait for a better time.

———

RICK SAUNDERS'S DAD squeezed his big hand around his son's arm and gently led him out of the funeral home. Everyone else at the wake had been crying. Rick had just stood there and stared.

"I'm worried about you, son," he said as he steered Rick in between two parked cars. "Are you feeling okay?"

"I'm fine, Dad. Everything's fine."

But everything wasn't fine. Mr. Saunders could see that. It wasn't like Rick not to show any feelings. He was holding everything in. A good friend had killed herself. Rick was in a daze.

Mr. Saunders decided to take Rick deer hunting. Just the two of them out there in the fresh air and woods. It would do Rick good. He'd relax and get his mind off things. Maybe he'd even talk about the suicide. He needed to talk.

MR. SAUNDERS WALKED on ahead. He'd stake out the area north of the stream; Rick would keep watch of the area south. Rick sat perfectly still, holding his high-powered rifle loosely in his hands. There was nothing to do but sit and wait and think. Words to a popular song kept running through his mind: "Roses never fade, and memories remain." Memories of going out of his way to irritate her. Walking by her lunch table and kicking her chair really hard. Spinning her around. Now he felt guilty. Maybe she had killed herself because of him. Maybe all the mean things he had done finally had gotten to her. He hadn't meant to hurt her. It was all just a game. Hadn't she seen that? Rick looked down at the rifle resting in his hands. It would be so easy. No one around to stop him.

RICK TRIED to act normal. He didn't want anyone to know how depressed he was. His friends and teachers had been through enough. They didn't need another suicidal teenager on their hands. But he was suicidal, and he had a plan. He didn't go for the car thing the way *she* had. That was too slow. He might change his mind. No, he wouldn't sit in a car and wait to die. Instead, he'd take all kinds of drugs—anything mixed—and then shoot himself to finish things off. He didn't want to end up a vegetable. He would do it right. He started writing his good-bye notes.

One of the first people he wrote to was "The Sarge." The Sarge was the head of the school's ROTC program and had been a friend for almost three years. Rick looked up to The Sarge; he was confident, strong, and wise. He also was very involved with the kids in ROTC. When Rick left his rifle out on the shooting range soon after the funeral, The Sarge was alarmed.

"It's not like you to forget to put your rifle back after target practice," he said.

"My mind was on something else, sir."

"Anything wrong?"

"No, sir. I was just thinking about the article I'm writing for the school paper."

He couldn't tell The Sarge how unhappy he was. He didn't want to disappoint him.

Rick wrote for the school newspaper. After Karen's suicide, he wrote an article about her and how her death could have been prevented, hoping it would make him feel less guilty. It didn't. Ms. Applebaum, the paper's faculty advisor, appreciated his efforts. She knew how hard it must have been for him. She felt she could count on him to single out anyone who seemed severely depressed because of the suicide.

The counseling department at Rick's high school made it easy to schedule an appointment. Anyone who wanted to see a counselor filled out a printed form, choosing from a checklist of problems. Rick wrote down the name *Karen* and shoved the form into his counselor's mail slot. He did that three days in a row. Mr. Sanchez, his counselor, must have thought it was some kind of joke. He never got in touch with Rick until it was almost too late.

Rick got along fine with his parents. The only child, he had everything he wanted—his own TV set, stereo, and phone. But he couldn't talk to his parents, not about this. They'd never understand. They'd tell him that his depression would pass, that there was nothing to worry about. Besides, his mother would get all emotional. She'd probably start crying or screaming or both. He didn't want to upset her. He loved her too much.

But he had to talk to someone. He felt like a pressure cooker. There had to be someone who would listen without getting hysterical. He didn't want to be lectured about how foolish he was. He just wanted someone to understand. Then he remembered Jenny, a friend on his ROTC squad.

So he flagged her down in the hall during a break.

"I've got to talk to you," he said.

"What's wrong?"

Rick breathed a sigh of relief. Jenny would listen. "I'm messed up," he said.

Jenny grabbed his arm and led him to an empty bench away from the other kids.

"What's the problem?"

Rick fidgeted with his notebook. Could he tell her?

"I'll listen, if you want to talk."

Okay. He'd tell her. "I'm going to kill myself."

Jenny bit the inside of her lip. "Do you have a plan?"

"Yeah. I'm not going to do it like *she* did. I couldn't handle that."

"Then how?" She couldn't believe that this was happening. She had just begun to sort out her own feelings since the funeral. Now this.

Rick lowered his voice. "I'm going to take all the drugs I can get my hands on. Then, when they start to work, I'm going to shoot myself."

Jenny wanted to scream but she stayed calm. "You're really serious, aren't you?"

"Yeah."

"You want to make sure you don't botch things up."

"I want to die."

"I know how you feel. I wanted to die, too."

"You did? You thought of killing yourself?"

"Just for a few minutes. Right after the funeral. But it wouldn't solve a thing."

"It will for me." Rick looked Jenny straight in the eyes. "Don't tell anyone."

She had to tell. She couldn't let another friend die.

"If you tell, I'm really going to kill myself. Then you'll have that on your conscience."

Jenny didn't answer. She just nodded her head.

"There's nothing you can do to change my mind. So don't try." He'd told her. He wasn't alone. But he was still depressed. Telling hadn't solved anything. He was worried about getting into college. Who would want him? Besides, Karen was dead.

Jenny was a wreck. What should she do? She didn't want Rick to hate her. But she didn't want him to die. Maybe she should tell The Sarge. He cared about Rick. But he'd had enough trouble helping the other kids during this whole disaster. Who else could she tell? Not Rick's parents. She didn't know them well enough. Not Ms. Applebaum. She wouldn't believe her. She had no choice: She'd have to tell The Sarge.

Jenny went to The Sarge before school started the next morning. He was flabbergasted. Rick? Thinking of suicide? He grabbed her hand, and the two of them raced down to the principal's office. Jenny repeated everything she had told The Sarge. Concerned, the principal picked up the phone and called Rick's counselor.

Rick was surprised when Mr. Sanchez called him to his office. He'd given up on ever seeing him.

"We haven't talked in a long time," Mr. Sanchez said as Rick sat down in his office.

He could say that again.

"How are you feeling these days?"

Rick stared down at his hands folded on his lap. "Okay." He didn't want to talk about his plan.

"You seem a bit down. People are concerned."

"Yeah . . . I guess they should be. You almost had another suicide on your hands."

Mr. Sanchez leaned forward. "Want to talk about it?"

"I'm real worried about getting into college. I want to go to Wisconsin, but I don't think I have a chance."

"Well, let's take a look at your grades," Mr. Sanchez said, pulling Rick's file out of his desk drawer.

He couldn't believe how easy it was to fool him.

"Your grades look pretty good." He took out his calculator and pushed a few keys. "Close to a *B* average. Not bad. I don't think you'll have any trouble."

What a pushover.

Mr. Sanchez droned on. "Now, you may want to consider applying to a couple of other schools, just in case."

Rick nodded. He wanted Mr. Sanchez to think he was listening. Actually, he was composing a good-bye note to his Uncle Ken.

Jenny was writing a note, too. She wanted to set the record straight. She wanted Rick to know what a dear friend he was. She wanted him to know how much she valued his friendship and his opinions. If he killed himself, she wrote, nothing he had ever said would mean a thing. He'd be one big fake in her eyes. Rick hated fakes. Maybe knowing that she would label *him* as one would stop him.

Rick's mother knew things weren't right. His grades had dropped. Nothing seemed to interest him anymore. He'd come home, go straight to his room, turn on the TV, and sit for hours without moving. What should she do? Should she call Dr. Lansky? Maybe Rick would talk to him. He sure wasn't opening up to her. But what if she was jumping to conclusions? What if he wasn't really that depressed? He'd hate her for interfering in his life. She didn't want that. Rick was her only child. He was all she had.

Jenny jumped when the phone rang. "Hello," she said, her heart pounding.

"Jenny?" the voice on the other end said.

"Yes, this is Jenny." She had no idea who it was.

"This is Mrs. Saunders, Rick's mother."

Why was she calling her?

"I'm worried about Rick. He just isn't himself these days. Has he said anything to you?"

Jenny didn't know what to do. Should she tell Mrs. Saunders the truth? "We've talked," she said hesitantly.

"What has he told you? I've got to know."

"He's not very happy," she said.

"It's because of that Jones girl, isn't it?"

"That, and a lot of other things." Why was she telling her this?

There was silence at the other end of the phone.

"I think he needs help," Jenny said. It wasn't enough.

"Has he talked about doing something like *she* did?"

"Yes," Jenny whispered.

"My God!"

Jenny wanted to crawl into a hole.

"I've got to call Rick's doctor right away. I won't let him hurt himself. I couldn't bear that." She was crying now. "I appreciate you telling me all this, Jenny."

Should she say "You're welcome"? The click on the other end saved her from having to decide.

Jenny sat holding the phone. Had she done the right thing? Rick had warned her not to say a word. He'd said he'd kill himself for sure if she did. She'd never forgive herself if he went ahead with it.

BY THE TIME Rick's dad came home that evening, all the arrangements had been made. Rick would be hospitalized the next afternoon for tests and observation. It was the only option. He couldn't be trusted, feeling the way he did. He might do something terrible. Alarmed, his dad took Rick's pistol apart and hid it. Then he took the trigger from Rick's rifle. Opening every drawer in his son's room, he searched for ammunition. He found it everywhere, stuffed under sweaters, shoved into corners. Rick wasn't taking any chances. How could he plan such a thing? Didn't he have everything he wanted?

Jenny couldn't concentrate on her homework. She kept thinking about the phone call. Would Rick's mother tell him about it? That would be the end of their friendship. Maybe the end of him. Her head throbbed as she thought about the last weeks. Her whole world had been turned inside out. First Karen, now Rick. How could she stop the madness? If she couldn't fight it, why not join them? Not her. She would never kill herself. She wasn't sure why. She just knew she wouldn't. Maybe she was a coward. The thought of dying scared her enough. The thought of taking her own life terrified her. It wasn't that she was religious or anything like that. No one had pounded it into her head that suicide was a sin. She just believed that problems could be solved. Things always got better. Sure, there was pain. A lot of it sometimes. But the pain would end. She was sure of that. She was only seventeen. She had her whole life in front of her. So did Rick. But he had lost the will to go on. She agreed that a person had the right to kill him- or herself. But having the right and actually going ahead with it were two different things. God, she hoped Rick would change his mind. Couldn't he see how much she cared? Didn't her friendship count for something?

When the phone rang this time, it rang four times before she got up the nerve to answer.

"Hello?" she said nervously.

"Jenny?"

It was Rick's mother again. What did she want? Had

something happened? "Yes," she said, her stomach tied up in knots.

"We're putting Rick in the hospital tomorrow. It's for the best."

He was alive. "That's great," Jenny said, realizing only after she'd said it how stupid she must have sounded.

"I want to thank you again for all your help." Then Mrs. Saunders's voice began to quiver. "I just hope the doctors can bring him out of this."

"I'm sure they can," Jenny said. She hoped she sounded sincere.

"YOUR FATHER and I have talked to Dr. Lansky. We've decided to put you into the hospital for some tests."

"The hospital?" Rick put the glass of milk he'd poured down on the kitchen counter. "The hospital?" he asked again.

"We're worried about you, son. You've been talking about killing yourself."

"Who told you that?" he asked angrily. "Whoever it was, they were lying."

"We're not going to take any chances. If the doctors don't think it's serious, you can come home in a few days."

He made a mental note: He would fool the doctors just the way he'd fooled Mr. Sanchez. He'd be out of that hospital in no time.

Jenny sat in her last class, watching the second hand on the wall clock move from one black mark to the next. This was all her fault. If she hadn't been so honest and said how troubled Rick really was, his mother might have backed off. But she couldn't lie. Rick *was* in bad shape.

Two-thirty. He'd be home by now, getting ready to go to the hospital. What would it be like? Would Rick be surrounded by glazed-eyed robots who'd had one too many electric-shock treatments? That would make him want to kill himself for sure. The suspense was killing her, too. Slowly.

RICK SLAMMED his bedroom door behind him. If he only had the guts, he'd get his rifle and end it all right now. But he wasn't ready yet. He hadn't finished all of his good-bye notes. And he needed to talk to Jenny. Jenny. She was the one, wasn't she? She'd gone and told his mother everything. He wanted to hate her, and part of him did. She hadn't kept his secret. But another part of him felt relieved. She cared about him. She didn't want him to die. Deep down, he knew he needed help. If only Karen hadn't killed herself, everything would be fine, he thought. Or would it? He didn't know anymore. But one thing was for sure: He was going to fool all those hotshot doctors. There was no way they were going to keep him in there for long.

Rick felt like an observer as he and his parents drove to the hospital. This wasn't really happening to him but to someone who looked just like him. He watched as this double checked into the psychiatric ward, kissed his parents good-bye, and was led to the room where he'd be staying. Rick felt sorry for the young man who sat down on the bed. He looked lost. The room, with its painted cement-block walls and sparse furniture, was like a glorified jail. How could anyone get well staying in a place like this?

Rick didn't worry about getting well. He only worried about how to convince the staff to let him go home.

Soon after he arrived, he was taken into a small

room with a computer and asked to answer each question as it appeared on the screen. One of the first questions read: "Have you ever left your body?" Rick shivered. How did they know? Had they seen him looking at himself in the lobby? Or was this a trick to get him to admit he was crazy? They couldn't fool him. He was too smart for that. Nervously, he typed in "N-O." The rest of the questions got easier. "Do you ever wake up and think that life isn't worth living?" "N-O." "Does a person have the right to take his or her own life?" "N-O." "Are you sometimes troubled by problems you can't solve?" He started to answer "no," then stopped. He didn't want to look too good. The doctors might get suspicious. Sure, he had some problems. Didn't everyone? Nothing wrong with a few problems. He typed in "Y-E-S." By the end of the questionnaire, he was sure he'd be out of the hospital soon.

He was right. After talking to several doctors and being observed for three days, Rick was released. He was not a serious risk to himself, they said. He was a strong kid who had hit bottom after his friend's suicide. He'd pull through.

Rick prayed that the kids at school wouldn't act overly nice to him. That would make him feel very uncomfortable. If they'd just be themselves—that would be a big help. And Jenny . . . he would have to face Jenny. She'd sent him the note while he was in the hospital. He'd read it over and over again until he knew it by heart. There was one sentence, the one about valuing his opinions. Each time he read it, he felt better. She actually thought he was a worthwhile person. She really did like him. And he liked her, too, even if she had told his mother. He'd probably have done the same thing, if the situation had been reversed.

The first day back at school was a rough one. Rick was sure that everyone he passed in the hall knew he'd been in a psychiatric hospital. They were looking at him funny, as if he were some kind of freak. Or were they? It was impossible to know for sure. One thing he did know for sure: If Jenny hadn't been there for him, he'd never have made it.

"I can't explain it," he said to her during lunch. "I don't know what it is, but you're the only person who really helps me."

Jenny smiled. She was thrilled to have her friend back.

"I don't want to pressure you," he said, "but knowing you're here makes all the difference."

Jenny nodded. She understood how important she was to him. It felt good, but scary, too. He depended on her. She couldn't let him down. "I'm glad you're back," she said.

"Me, too." His voice shook as he talked.

She put her arm around him. "You seem very nervous."

"Wish I could say everything is just dandy, but I've still got problems to face."

"Right now, over a peanut-butter-and-jelly sandwich?" she asked.

He didn't want to laugh. Not now. Not after what he'd been through. But before he knew it, he was laughing hysterically.

"I can't stop," he gasped, wrapping his arms around his sides. "I can't stop!"

"Then don't," Jenny said. They would have to laugh more often.

MOST DEPRESSED TEENS don't want to die. All they really want is a friend. Rick was lucky. Jenny was there to listen, to mirror, to reflect Rick's feelings without lecturing or making judgments. Rick meant it when he said, ". . . knowing you're here makes all the difference."

Kids who threaten suicide aren't interested in ending their lives. They're interested in ending their pain. Suicide is a cry for help, and you can help. If a friend is suicidal, you could well be the first to know. If you don't think your friend should be left alone, don't leave. Stay with him/her until an adult whom you contact—a teacher, parent, doctor, or policeman—arrives.

If, however, you think your friend can be left alone, but needs to talk to someone, a scenario might go something like this:

"This seems bigger than we can handle. How about talking to someone?"

"Oh, I'll be okay."

"I'm worried about you. I want you to get some help."

"Really, I'm fine. I feel a lot better."

"I'm glad you feel better. But your problems are still there."

"I won't kill myself . . . I promise."

"Promise to talk to someone, too?"

"I promise."

"I care about you a lot."

"I know you do."

*Suicide-Prevention Centers*

How do you find the closest suicide-prevention center? Call 411, "0," 911, or look in the Yellow Pages under *Suicide, Crisis, Mental Health,* or *Counseling.* In a nonemergency, you can call the American Association of Suicidology at 303-692-0985. A staff member will refer you to the nearest center.

There are more than two hundred suicide-prevention centers throughout the United States. Most of them have twenty-four-hour, seven-day-a-week emergency telephone service. Some have their own rescue squads to help people after they've attempted suicide. While most centers offer help by telephone only, some have professionals on staff who will counsel someone in trouble.

*Community Mental Health Clinics*

Community mental health clinics are listed in the Yellow Pages under *Mental Health.* If you or a friend has trouble finding one, you can call the National Mental Health Association at 703-684-7722.

These nonprofit, publicly supported centers serve people within a certain area. Most of them have one or two psychiatrists on staff, several psychologists, social workers, counselors, and alcohol and drug-abuse specialists. These clinics usually set their fees on a sliding scale: A patient pays according to the family's income.

*Hospitals*

All hospitals connected with medical schools and those with more than two hundred beds have departments of psychiatry, social work departments, and, frequently, adolescent clinics.

Many hospitals (even some smaller ones) have a Crisis Line. If you or a friend needs help, call the nearest hospital Crisis Line. Tell them that you have an emergency and briefly describe the problem.

*Therapists*

There are plenty of psychiatrists and other therapists in this country. The trick is to find one who specializes in working with adolescents and who has had experience working with suicidal teens. Often, your family doctor is a good person to ask for names. Sometimes, someone you know is seeing a therapist who comes highly recommended. Or you can call the American Psychiatric Association at 202-682-6000, the American Psychological Association at 202-955-7600, or the National Association of Social Workers at 202-565-0333.

*Teachers*

Teachers spend more time with their students than parents do. They are often more aware of what is really going on in a teenager's life. If you or a friend has a favorite teacher, turning to him or her can be a good idea.

CONCLUSION

You and your friends can be the best weapon against the increase in teenage suicides. Friends usually talk to other friends before opening up to a parent or teacher. You might be the first to know if a friend is thinking about suicide.

You can help. You can encourage a friend who is depressed to talk to you, if you feel comfortable, or to someone else. You can find out what the problems are and how seriously your friend is thinking about suicide. You can show you care by listening, mirroring, and asking good questions. And you can stay with your friend until professional help is found.

IF ONLY BRAD, Teri, Steve, and the thousands of other teens who took their own lives had had you as a friend. They might still be alive.

# *Suggested Reading*

NONFICTION

Bolton, Iris. *My Son . . . My Son.* Belmore Way, GA: Bolton Press, 1983.

Dinkmeyer, Don, and McKay, Gary. *The Parent's Guide: Step/Teen Systematic Training for Effective Parenting.* Circle Pines, MN: American Guidance Service, 1983.

Griffin, M.D., Mary and Felsenthal, Carol. *A Cry For Help: Exploring and Exploding the Myths About Teenage Suicide-A Guide for All Parents and Adolescents.* New York: Doubleday & Company, Inc. 1983

Hyde, Margaret, and Forsythe, Elizabeth. *Suicide: The Hidden Epidemic.* New York: Franklin Watts, 1978.

Klagsbrun, Francine. *Too Young to Die: Youth and Suicide.* New York: Pocket Books, 1981.

Langone, John. *Dead End: A Book About Suicide.* Boston/Toronto: Little, Brown and Company, 1983

Mack, John, and Hickler, Holly. *Vivienne: The Life and Suicide of an Adolescent Girl.* Boston/Toronto: Little, Brown and Company, 1981.

FICTION

Arrick, Fran. *Tunnel Vision.* Scarsdale, NY: Bradbury Press, 1980.

Gerson, Corinne. *Passing Through.* New York: Dial Press, 1978.

Green, Hannah. *I Never Promised You a Rose Garden.* New York: Holt, Rinehart, Winston, 1964.

Guest, Judith. *Ordinary People.* New York: Penguin, 1982.

Peck, Robert. *Remembering the Good Times.* New York: Delacorte, 1985.

Plath, Sylvia. *The Bell Jar.* New York: Bantam Books, 1975.